EXCEED LIMITS AND BREAK BARRIERS

UNDERSTANDING THE POWER OF WORDS

DOUGLAS PYSZKA

ISBN: 0-9993844-2-2
ISBN-13: 978-0-9993844-2-8

CONTENTS

ACKNOWLEDGMENTS

SPECIAL THANKS

I want to acknowledge and give special thanks to my Lord and Savior Jesus, whom I love with all my heart, My Father God, who is so good to me and His Holy Spirit who has empowered me to complete this project.

Also, I am thankful for my wonderful loving wife Fiona. Together, we are an explosive force for God in this earth. I am grateful for the love and support she gives me in serving God together. She is amazing.

I am very grateful for my two sons, Gabriel and Josiah. I am blessed to be the father of such wonderful sons. I am excited to pass onto them a godly heritage. They are amazing boys. Thank you for allowing me to dedicate extra time to complete this project.

Thanks to Lisa Schmidt, our faithful and diligent administrative coordinator who helped me dot the "I's" and cross the "T's". Your input is greatly appreciated.

I am grateful for the congregation of Victory Christian Fellowship. I am greatly blessed to be able to oversee such a wonderful, loving group of people.

INTRODUCTION

This book was written under the direction and inspiration of God's Holy Spirit. It is designed to help anyone to exceed the limits of your life and to break through barriers that have hindered you or held you back. Every person faces restrictions, challenges, enemies and difficulties but you do not have to accept them as the end. They are subject to change and move out of your way. All of us are equipped to overcome these things and transform our lives with the help, influence and power of God, not on our own.

The key to moving forward and going beyond your imagination is in your mouth, tongue and heart. The words you say and how you say them are important and instrumental in whether you succeed or fail. Your mouth speaks what is in your heart. If you desire to transform your life, you must change the content of your heart by depositing God's Word in your heart, then speaking God's words boldly, confidently and with certainty. When God's Word is spoken, situations are changed, limits are removed, and doors open to greater things.

Jesus is the ultimate role model of great speech. No other person's words had a greater impact on people and things in the earth than Jesus' words. His words are Spirit and life, originating from a different kingdom and bringing true life to everything and everyone. He spoke to both people and things and everything He said brought about a change. He authorized everyone who believes in Him to speak impactful words also. When your words agree and are aligned with the Lord's words, you will see miracles, signs and wonders wherever you go. Get ready to exceed limits and break barriers.

1 EXCEED LIMITS THROUGH THE POWER OF WORDS

Understanding the Power of Words

Limits and barriers are in the way of every person's success, but you are fully equipped to exceed limits and break barriers. The key to surpassing restrictions in life and overcoming obstacles is in your mouth, but you must understand the power that words have. Antony Farindon, a minister from the 17th century said, "Our words are the commentaries of our wills."

Words are powerful and with them you can overcome obstacles, conquer foes, create your future, and cause you to triumph in life. The U.S.A. came into being through the Declaration of Independence and Constitution, two documents full of words. Words will clear your pathway or clog your progress. Yes, words are the key to overcoming challenges or being overcome by them.

Words can persuade people to act in a good way or bad way. Lawyers make arguments with words designed to convince juries and judges to decide in their favor. Speeches use specific words, spoken in a certain way to inspire their audience. Many speeches have changed history and are remembered long after they were given.

You can be comforted with words when you are sad or disappointed. Words can encourage you to keep going when you are down. Have you ever received or given a "pep talk"? It gives you the advantage and motivation to press on. There are people you trust to advise you with in making good choices. Words from teachers help you learn, words from mentors give you direction and words help nations govern their people through laws.

You can also connect with God through words when you pray, worship, read, hear preaching, express your feelings and convey your thoughts to Him. Everything that happens in your life is connected to the words you speak every day. Are you convinced that words are powerful? They are.

God wants you to consider the words you use and the conversations you engage in daily. What do you say about yourself, about others and about circumstances of life? Would you like to be spoken to by someone using the same words that you use? Jesus desires to enhance your speech so you will speak like a king with authority and power just like Him.

John 6:63 describes the words that Jesus spoke as Spirit and life. His words described a spiritual kingdom. God's Holy Spirit guided Him in what to say and His words were a lifeline and hope to those who were dead in trespasses and sins. All of Jesus' words are life-changing, uplifting and true. His words are so powerful that no one could argue against Him, contradict Him or deceive Him. The religious leaders of His day tried many times and failed each time. He is the best speaker who says everything in the most excellent way and the best example to follow. Every believer has access to God's Holy Spirit, who helps them choose good words and filter their speech. You are defeated or victorious through your words.

God, who is Omnipotent, omniscient and omni-present created the universe with words. He could have made the world any way that He wanted to, but He chose to do it by speaking words. God conceived how the universe should be in His mind. He looked and saw barriers that were blocking the earth from taking shape.

In the first chapter of Genesis, God looked at the limits on the earth, having no form, desolation and darkness. What would God do to change what He saw?

How would God break through these barriers? **He spoke words** to shape and form the world into what He wanted it to be. Those were powerful words. God used four words to form and fashion the cosmos, "Let there be light." When God uttered these words, creation responded to what He said, light began to be and has not stopped being. Do you think that you can fashion your life with your words? Yes, you can.

You need to know that the words you say and how you utter them matter. Whether you realize it or not, your words are creating something good or bad in your life. There is a spiritual force operating behind every word you speak. Spoken words are significant and will produce either negative or positive results. Your speech either produces life or death; peace or trouble; health or sickness; hope or despair; joy or sadness; confusion or wisdom; truth or lies. By your words you are limited and by your words you can exceed limits. Words that come from God are designed to break down barriers and shake worlds.

Have you considered why you use the words that you do? What you say every day reveals what you look at, listen to, lean on and like. It is what you have been marinating in, meditating on and captivated by. What you see, hear and experience in your environment gets into your heart and comes out of your mouth. Your mouth is the exhaust of what has been fueling your heart. The good news is you can change your words by allowing God's Word into your heart. When you put something different in your heart, you will say different words and your circumstances will improve.

Your words are either on the side of light or darkness. What you say either reflects your encounter with the Light of the World, Jesus, or what you encounter from the devil in darkness where he attempts to steal, kill and destroy. Both the devil and God listen to you speak, and what you say determines whose presence is active and operating in your life. The devil shows up to steal from you, kill you and destroy you when you use negative, evil, fearful and doubtful words. God shows up to bless you, lead you and help you to breakthrough obstacles that are in your way when you use positive, righteous, true and faith-filled words. Choose what you say about anything wisely.

Honestly consider the words that come out of your mouth and see if the limits you face have any connection to the words you speak. If you are not able to accurately evaluate your words, ask a close friend to help you. They may be able to point out the type of words that you use each day. Remember, words create limits or exceed limits. To surpass limits, you must speak different words. If you want to live an unlimited life, then speak words that support that desire and are rooted in God's Word. Also, look at things that may be impeding your progress. You can say something to them. Jesus overcame obstacles all the time and

He has empowered you to do the same, just use your mouth and speak His words.

Jesus Exceeded Limits and Broke Barriers with His Words

Here are few ways that Jesus demonstrated how powerful words are. He spoke to a fig tree saying, "May no one eat fruit from you again." His disciples heard Him say this and the next day they saw how the tree obeyed when they found that it was dried up from the roots, Mark 11:12-14. Jesus cursed a tree and the tree died. That was no coincidence, that was a result of what He said. Are there some things that appear fruitful in your life, but upon closer inspection, you find no fruit? What can you say to change your fruitlessness? Some things in your life may need to be cursed to die and other things may need to be told to live and thrive.

Jesus spoke to a storm. He told a storm what it needed to do. He rebuked the wind and said to the sea, "Silence! Be still!" The wind ceased and there was a great calm. His disciples acknowledged that the wind and the sea obeyed Him, Mark 4:39-41. Has any chaos or trouble suddenly appeared in your life? What are you saying about it? You can calm it with your words just like Jesus did.

Jesus spoke to broken body parts. Jesus told a man with a withered hand to stretch out his hand. As the man stretched forth his hand it was completely restored to normal, Matthew 13:13. When Jesus spoke, He spoke God's Words. You may think, that was Jesus and I'm not Jesus. If you believe in Jesus, you can say what He said. You can speak God's Words too. Do you have any health issues? How do you speak about them? Are you speaking life and health to them or do you repeat what the symptoms tell you? Speak life and healing to your physical body. God's Word has much to say about healing, find out what it says and then you say what is written.

Jesus even spoke to men who were dead. Jesus stood before His friend's tomb and said to the dead man, "Lazarus, come out!" Lazarus came out wrapped in his grave cloths, John 11:43-44. Have you given up on any of your dreams or goals? What needs to come out of you to make you successful? Call it out.

What Jesus said changed these circumstances and made them better than what they were. If you would like to change any of your circumstances in life, you can do what Jesus did, and boldly speak a Scripture that relates to your situation and watch it change. You may wonder, what if it doesn't change the moment I say it? Keep saying it until it changes, that is the perseverance and determination of faith. You will learn more about how you can change your situations with your words as you read on.

You Have a Mouth to Move Mountains

There are two main components that work together to move obstacles when you speak, your heart and your mouth. They function like a motor and a transmission in a vehicle. A motor makes the car run and the transmission moves it forward and backward. A vehicle with a motor and no transmission will simply idle and not be able to go anywhere.

Just like a transmission and a motor are essential to a vehicle, both your heart and mouth are necessary to move mountains. What is in your heart will come out of your mouth whether it is good or bad. For example, if your heart contains fear, then you will speak fear-based words like, "I'm afraid; I can't; I'm too small; I'm nobody; and It's too tough..." If your heart is full of faith, then you will speak faith-filled words like, "I can; I'm able; I'm healed; I will obey; and I'm a winner..." The results you want to have in life need to mirror the images you have in your heart and the words you speak out of your mouth. They must all agree.

In Mark 11:22-25, Jesus encouraged those who believe in Him to have faith in God. Those who have faith are to **speak to mountains**. Is He talking about actual mountains in the earth or something else? Mountains represent the limits and obstacles that are in your way that block your progress and keep you from what God has given you. To remove a mountain in your way you must speak to it, use your words and say, "Mountain, get out of my way and go into the sea!"

Here is the catch about moving mountains. When you speak to a mountain, you must not doubt in your heart. If there is any doubt in your heart, it will be heard in your words. If you doubt what you said, the mountain will not respond. You must believe what you say will happen just as you said it. Your belief in your words is like gunpowder in a cannon. Just like the gunpowder is the power that launches the cannon ball, your belief in what you say is the power to bring it to pass. If your progress is hindered in any way, there is probably a mountain that needs to be removed so you can continue moving forward and taking ground.

Moses spoke to a mountain. Moses was sent by God into Egypt to deliver God's people from slavery. The *mountain* in his way that was hindering progress was the king of Egypt, Pharaoh. Moses spoke to his *mountain*, Pharaoh, and said, "Let my people go!" He spoke with authority and confidence. God backed up Moses' words and performed ten incredible plagues that led to Israel's deliverance. After these things, the Egyptian ruler let God's people go and Israel was set free just like Moses said. Jesus said to cast your mountain into the sea. Pharaoh also *drowned in the sea* where he was seen no more. Speaking to your mountain as Jesus said works.

Abraham spoke to a mountain, his childlessness. God promised Abraham that he would be a father of many nations. He and his wife Sarah never had children, and Sarah was in her sixties and Abraham in his seventies. God changed Abraham's name from Abram to Abraham, signifying he was changed. God added something extra to his name. Abraham means father of many nations. Once God spoke this name, Abraham believed God and he started telling everyone his new name.

Abraham told many people that he was a father of many nations. Twenty-five years after God promised Abraham he would be a father, he and Sarah had a son when they were in their ninety's. The mountain of childlessness was removed as Abraham spoke God's Word to it.

David spoke to a mountain. His mountain was a soldier that stood over nine feet tall. David spoke to that giant and said he was going to defeat him in battle. David beat Goliath with his words before he beat him in battle. The giant was defeated and removed out of the way just as David said. You will find out more about David under the *Winning with Words* chapter.

These three examples show you how to move your mountain –

you use words and speak to it. Find out what God says in His Word about the mountain you are facing. Then speak what God said about it and do not doubt in your heart, believe that what you say will happen and it must move.

A strong belief moves mountains and speaks with confidence, assurance, boldness and authority. These qualities are a few of the characteristics of faith and can be heard in how you speak. You can strengthen your belief by knowing what the Bible says, believing it and standing on it no matter what.

The Word of God is a weapon of both offense and defense. When fear, doubt and unbelief attack and try to overwhelm you, *defend yourself with the Word*. Say something like, "I resist fear, I believe, I trust God and what He said, what God said is so!" You must battle fear, doubt and unbelief with opposing words, and God's Word is the only weapon you need to both defend and attack these opponents. You will soon see that what you say will be produced in your life.

2 DISCERN BETWEEN POSITIVE AND NEGATIVE WORDS

You get to choose to use positive words or negative words about every area of life.

Your words are like a battery having both a positive and negative side. The words you choose to use will determine whether the results you have in life are positive or negative. To see the difference between the two, let's compare them face to face. You are equipped and able to identify appropriate from inappropriate words, and God will teach you what to say and how to say it by His Spirit. He will show you what positive words you are to say that best deal with your situation. As you choose to make God's Words your words, you will get into God's success plan for your life.

Proverbs chapter 15 demonstrates the difference between positive and negative words. Positive words benefit and bless you, while negative words harm and punish you. When you speak positive words, you have God's favor working for you. When you speak negative words, you give the devil permission to steal, kill and destroy. Seeing what results come from spoken words may help you change what you say and help you speak in a better way.

Positive words are gentle words, but **negative words are harsh words**. Gentle words benefit your soul. Gentle words are peaceful, mild and soothing, they calm intense atmospheres and cause anger to subside.

Harsh words are rough, aggressive and demanding, they ignite anger and stir up wrath. If you speak harsh words you will provoke people instead of inspiring them. Most people despise harsh words, Proverbs 15:1. Insert chapter two text here. Insert chapter two text here. Insert chapter two text here.

Wise words are positive words, but **foolish words are**

negative words. Wisdom is a good benefit. When you speak wise words, you speak like God, for God is wise. Wisdom attracts and increases in knowledge. A fool repels knowledge and decreases his knowledge. A wise person loves to learn and cares about others.

A fool has no such desire. **Foolish words are stupid words**. A fool despises learning, that is why he speaks stupid words, and is forever limited until he stops his foolishness. A fool is selfish and does not care about anyone but himself. God laughs at fools because they say He does not exist.

The way to distinguish between a fool and a wise man is to listen to what they say. A wise man **speaks words of understanding and knowledge**. A fool **speaks words that are near destruction**. Your words reveal the real you. Words either exceed limits and break barriers; or set limits and hinder progress. The righteous are unlimited and **speak words that are wise** and acceptable to God. The wicked are limited and **speak words that are perverse and twisted**. Proverbs 10:13; 10:31-32

The proud speech of a fool brings a rod of discipline, but the lips of the wise protect them. A virtuous woman opens her mouth with wisdom and on her tongue is the law of kindness, Proverbs 14:3; 31:26. A promiscuous woman opens her mouth with persistent pleading and flattering talk to seduce senseless men, Proverbs 7.

Positive words promote health and life, but **negative words promote deceit, perversity and grief**. Health and life are good benefits. Jesus' positive words promoted health and life wherever He went, and He made people better by improving the quality of their life. The words of Jesus brought forgiveness to sinners and gave them a chance to have eternal life. All who continue to carry the Lord's message today promote health and life wherever they go also.

Satan is the father of lies and the author of deception. Lies and deception pervert and twist the truth. Believing a lie restricts and limits your life causing great grief. No one likes to be deceived after realizing what they believed was not true or based on lies. Those who are deceived do not think that their situation can change. Even God's people perish for a lack of knowledge.

Positive words bring joy, negative words bring sorrow. Joy is a great benefit. Words affect the atmosphere of a place because words are powerful. When you are full of joy, you speak joy-filled exuberant words. As joy increases and overflows, it must express itself in some way. You may laugh, sing, dance or shout, etc., to express the joy that fills you. That will affect your environment in a positive way and may cause others to experience that joy too.

When you are full of sadness, you speak sorrowful words that lead to depression. Sad people look down, away from people. Sad people don't smile. Some people may cry at a funeral even though they did not intend to because sadness permeates the atmosphere. Sadness negatively affects atmospheres.

Determine what kind of atmosphere you would like to have and speak appropriate words that will create the environment you desire. Both joy and sadness are contagious, and people are affected by every type of word you speak. This is not saying you should never be sad. If all you do is focus on sad things and speak sad words and never change your input or output, the negative atmosphere you created can turn into a deep depression. You can change your words to change your current atmosphere.

Positive words prevent fights, but **negative words pick fights**. The ability to stop a fight is a great benefit. Hot-tempered, vengeful and angry words start fights and cause you to lose your composure. Words can cause anger to rise or they can cause anger to subside. These types of words require no thinking, only reaction. A hot-tempered, vengeful and angry mindset is controlled by the sin nature and causes you to do things you regret later.

Cool-tempered words are gentle, peaceful and quiet, and can extinguish strife, quench contention and bring an end to a fight, Proverbs 15:18. Which temperature setting is your mouth set at, cool or hot? We are supposed to fight the devil, not each other. Know who the real enemy is.

Positive words agree with God and **are pleasant, but**

negative words disagree with God and are evil. God's agreement is a wonderful benefit. God is good, and He hates evil. The Lord favors pure and kind words. Pure words are kind, loving, gentle and sincere. They are helpful, correct wrongs, encourage those who may be lagging behind and refresh another's soul.

The Lord detests and strongly disagrees with evil plans, evil thoughts and evil words. If a person plans to murder, steal, gossip, commit adultery, lie, dishonor authority or anything like that, God is against it because it is evil. It goes against His Word, nature and character. It only leads to death. God provided us with positive alternatives to evil thoughts and He told us what to think on.

Positive words are righteous words, but **negative words are wicked words**. Being right with God is a great benefit. What is the difference between a righteous person and a wicked person? The difference between them is the content and condition of their heart and what they say. A righteous man has a heart that is right with God and he thinks about his words before he speaks because he desires to please God in everything he does. God is His ally and He hears this man's prayers.

A wicked man does not think about what he says because he does not desire to please God. He is free to blurt out evil words because he has an evil heart. Jesus is against a wicked man unless he is willing to repent, get right with God and make Jesus Lord of his life. A righteous man is rewarded for his righteousness and a wicked man is punished for his wickedness, Proverbs 15:28-29.

Positive changes occur from a man who appreciates wisdom, but negative changes occur from a man who is a wicked fool and despises wisdom. Positive changes benefit you well. A man who values wisdom responds positively to correction. When corrected, a wise man humbles himself, heeds the correction, repents with true sorrow and changes his behavior and attitude in a positive way.

A man who despises wisdom responds negatively to correction. When corrected, a fool puffs himself up with pride, acknowledges no wrongdoing on his part, blows off the correction and blames other things for his failure. God corrects His children out of love and how they respond to Him determines if they are wise or foolish.

Determine whether your words will be on a positive course to greatness or a negative course to destruction. You must decide to abide by God's standards of good speech that He set forth in His Word. He is not going to lower His standards.

A righteous mouth produces wisdom and speaks what is appropriate, but a perverse tongue brings destruction. Righteous words are rewarded, but perverse words are punished, Proverbs 10:31-32. God punishes the wicked by letting them have what they say. Words are like seeds and negative seeds sown lead to a negative harvest reaped. Build your vocabulary out of good words and you will overcome your enemy.

DOUGLAS PYSZKA

3 HOW YOU USE YOUR VOICE IS YOUR CHOICE

Are you a voice for God and what He represents or are you a voice for the devil and what he represents? God's side wins and the devil's side loses.

You get to choose which words you speak each day. It takes the same effort to speak negative words as it does to speak positive words. There is only one source of all positive words, the Bible. The sources of negative words are: the world, the flesh and the devil. All negative words are words that contradict God and what He says.

God's Word is the truth. The truth changes facts. Everything God says is true. What God says when He speaks and what is written in the Bible supersede or override any feeling, symptom, situation or opinion from anyone else. God says emphatically that you are healed, strengthened and restored. If you are sick and you hear what God said or read what He wrote in the Bible, in order to receive your healing, you must believe what you heard is true and confess, "I am healed." You are not denying your sickness, you are simply saying what God said about it. You and God agree on the same outcome, the truth. If you agree with your sickness it will not change. If you agree with God, your sickness will change and become healed. With God, your potential is unlimited.

If the words you speak agree more with your natural circumstances - your senses, feelings and experiences - than they agree with God, you will have problems in receiving what God said. You are saying what the Lord said is untrue. Basically, you are calling God a liar. Yet, it is impossible for God to lie.

If God says something different than what your natural situation says, you must choose who you believe and trust more. If you trust God, then say what He said, and your circumstance will be transformed. But, if you trust your physical conditions more, then all will remain the same. Believe God to become unbound.

The Bible records people who received healing, specifically by what they said - A Roman Centurion, Matt. 8, Jairus' daughter, Mk. 5 and a woman who had a blood issue also mentioned in Mark 5. What did they say? They said that Jesus was there only hope and answer relying on nothing else. In each example, Jesus responded positively and approved of their statements, and gave them miraculous results. They chose to believe God and speak words that agreed with and expressed their beliefs. People can also choose to disagree and doubt God.

Zechariah, John the Baptist's father, chose to disagree with God. He was a priest serving in the temple and God sent an angel to him to tell him good news. Although he and his wife Elizabeth were old in age, the angel announced to him that they would have a son and they were to name him John. This was a miracle!

When Zechariah heard what the angel spoke, he doubted God and did not believe it was possible. How do we know he doubted God? He responded to the angel saying, "How can I know this? I am an old man and my wife is advanced in years." After he wondered how this could be, he stated his age, which was his limit and barrier. Zechariah elevated his natural circumstances above what God said through the angel. The angel testified that he was sent to speak to Zechariah God's good news. Zechariah doubted it. **His heart and mouth expressed their disagreement to God's Word**. The angel told Zechariah that he would not be able to speak a word because he did not believe what God said. If Zechariah could have spoken his doubt-filled and unbelieving words, they may have negatively interfered with God's plan. So, Zechariah's mouth was shut not being able to speak a word for nine months. He suffered an inconvenient consequence of doubt and disbelief. His choice was to voice disbelief in God which closed his mouth for nine months. It was when he chose to believe what God said that his mouth was loosed, and he could speak again. The first words out of his mouth were praise to God, Luke 1:64.

Words are Fruit

Words are the fruit of your life. If you did not know anything about how to identify a fruit tree by its leaves or bark, how would you know how to identify which tree is which? The answer is to look at the fruit that it produces. Apple trees produce apples. Lemon trees produce lemons. Coconut trees produce coconuts, so on and so forth. Whether you are a negative tree or a positive tree is determined by which words you speak continually. Positive trees use good, uplifting, encouraging and truthful words. Negative trees use degrading, lying, deceitful and untrue words.

The Bible describes humans as good or bad trees in Matthew 12:33-37. Words are what make the tree good or bad. The words you speak every day, over everything, show everyone what kind of tree you are. Your words are the fruit that your roots produce. A person who has faith in God speaks faith-filled words that God has sanctioned and approved. Believers in Christ reverberate words that God has spoken in the Bible. An evil speaking person does not have faith in God and speaks words that are sanctioned by his flesh, the world and the devil. Speaking good, kind, loving and gentle words brings satisfaction and speaking bad, abrasive, harsh, foolish and false words brings destruction.

Just as trees have roots, the root of your life is your heart. Out of your heart flow the issues of life, Proverbs 4:23. Your mouth speaks whatever is in your heart. A good man brings good things out of the treasure of his heart. An evil man brings evil things out of the evil treasure of his heart.

Matthew Henry, a Bible commentator said, "The heart is the fountain, words are the streams. A troubled fountain, and a corrupt spring, must send forth muddy and unpleasant streams."

The difference between a good man and an evil man is the words that he speaks.

It is apparent that there are many people who are not concerned about the words they use or how they speak. People do not believe in or have knowledge of the power of words, so they speak negatively about many things, often unconsciously. They are bad trees. We live in world full of bad trees that distort speech.

God pays attention to your words and will hold you accountable for every idle word that you speak, Matthew 12:36-37. Strong's

Concordance defines an idle word as a lazy, thoughtless, unprofitable and injurious word. Basically, an idle word is one that does not do anything or help anyone in anyway. You could call it gibberish. God considers idle words evil, wicked and false. There are many idle words spoken in our world. Idle words limit you and block you from moving forward.

In Matthew 12:37 Jesus expressed how important words are by saying, "By your words you will be justified and by your words you will be condemned."

Young's Literal Translation says it like this, "For from thy words thou shalt be declared righteous, and from thy words thou shalt be declared unrighteous."

The difference between you being justified or condemned is the words you say. That is powerful! The words you use daily really determine the outcome of your life. A justified life is a free life, while a condemned life is a confined life. If you want to be justified, speak good, positive and godly words. If you want to be condemned, speak negative, false and evil words. Your words you use every day reveal what kind of person you are. Choose which type of fruit you want to produce.

To determine if you are a good tree, ask yourself, "Do my words line up with God's nature, character, heart? Are my words truthful, loving and kind? Is the Lord Jesus pleased with the words I use?" If there is any discrepancy between you and God, change your words and start saying His Words. Pray this prayer from Psalm 19:14, "May the words of my mouth and the meditation of my heart be pleasing in Your sight, Lord, my Rock and Redeemer."

Ephesians 4:25-32 gives you very clear commands on how to govern your speech. Stop lying, speak the truth. Don't use foul language when you speak. Use words that encourage and build up others. Stop saying vicious and hurtful words that are full of bitterness, anger, wrath and slander. Use merciful words to forgive others as God also forgave you in Christ. You are responsible for choosing the words you say and controlling your mouth. Your words make a big difference in your life.

The Lord Jesus Christ has authorized His followers to speak His Word while exercising wisdom in speaking. He will help you make your speech gracious, seasoning it with salt, causing it to bear good fruit. God will help you to say the right answer in the right way when you respond to others.

How Correction Improves the Quality of Your Fruit

The process of developing good fruit involves adjusting and correcting your course. How do you respond when you are corrected? Correction gives you an opportunity to change, to do what is right and start fresh. Coaches correct their players. Teachers correct their students. Parents correct their children. Managers correct their employees and God corrects His children. The purpose of correction is to enhance fruitfulness. Most people do not like to be corrected but we all need it at some point. Let's respond well when it happens.

God's goodness, wisdom and understanding comes upon the person who listens to life-giving correction. Those who disregard discipline despise themselves because they are not concerned about consequences until they experience loss and destruction. God lets them be ensnared in their own devices and ruined by their own words.

For example, not heeding correction limits the mercy you could receive. When Adam sinned, and God confronted him, he did not humble himself. He took no responsibility for his sin and he blamed the woman and God who gave her to him. He may have received more mercy if he had responded better to correction.

In 1 Samuel 15, God commanded King Saul to attack and destroy the Amalekites for the evil they did. He was not to spare any one, neither human nor animal. Saul attacked them but kept the Amalekite king alive along with the best of their herds and flocks. God confronted Saul through the prophet Samuel. Saul blamed the people for his sin. God called his actions rebellious, stubborn and evil and he lost the anointing from God to be king. He was still on the throne, but he did not have God's power on him and an evil spirit came to him and tormented him. All this happened because he did not heed correction. When you respond well to correction you exceed limits. If you do not regard correction, you will be restricted and limited, Proverbs 15:31.

Following are some practical ways to help you improve your speech and promote wisdom, righteousness and confidence in God. As you evaluate your words prepare to make changes. It is more effective to change your words before they come out of your mouth rather than after you have spoken them.

Think before You speak

American clergyman and writer, Maltbie Davenport Babcock said, "When I speak, let me think first. Is it true? Is it kind? Is it necessary? If not, let it be left unsaid."

If you have been traveling on the *negative word* avenue, you can exit from it and enter onto the *positive* expressway. Something that will help you change your course of negativity is to slow your speech. Don't be too hasty to answer but think about what you are going to say before you say it. It is easier to stop a negative word before it gets out than to recover from it after it leaves the mouth.

All of us have felt dumb or guilty for saying something without thinking, and each time it is embarrassing, uncomfortable and it makes you want to hide. You are often made fun of for saying such things. The Bible says, "There is more hope for a stupid fool than for someone who speaks without thinking." Proverbs 29:20 NLT. What is this proverb saying? A stupid fool can stop being foolish by not saying anything or he can gain wisdom. A person who speaks without thinking has a more difficult recovery because words are harder to change once they have been spoken. Their impact has already been felt and the damage is done. They can apologize, but the words got out. Words can't go back in your mouth once you speak them.

A fool has hope in that he can change. He can only go higher, but a person who answers too quickly must swallow his pride, admit his wrong and go on from there. People who can laugh at themselves recover more quickly from a misspoken word. You are more likely to outrun your limits by thinking before speaking.

Every one of us should pay more attention to the words we use every day. People consider what they will wear before they put it on, what they will eat before they get a meal, and we should consider what we say before we speak. *We must constantly consider our words before they leave our mouths.* A Christ follower should be quick to hear and slow to speak. We all have two ears and one mouth so we can listen twice as much as we speak, James 1:19. That is a good practical principle that we can implement right now.

Choose Words That Agree with God's Character and Nature

The Lord does not like, nor is He a fan of, negative words. Malachi 2:17 says, "You have wearied the Lord with your words." The people who heard this asked, "In what way have we wearied Him?" To weary the Lord is to wear out His patience with murmuring and discontent. God hates complaining. God did not want to hear anymore of their blasphemous words that were full of unbelief and mistrust. God is pleased when people believe Him and grieved when they doubt Him. God gets to a point where He is tired of hearing the negative speech. Parents feel the same way when their children continuously whine.

Apparently, the people in Malachi's day said that everyone who does evil is good in the sight of the Lord, and He delights in them. God does not delight in evil doers. They also asked, "Where is the God of justice?" They thought that God was giving a pass to the wicked, but He was not. Know that the wicked will be served justice by the Lord. The Lord sits on a throne founded on justice and righteousness. God hates lying, false testimony and one who spreads strife between people.

Those words that the people spoke were not true and by no means reflected the nature of God. God does not consider evil people good. God hates evil. The people who said these words did not choose their words wisely. The false words that the people said about God came out of hearts that were: faithless, disheartened by their circumstances, doubting God's provision and disbelieving His promises. The words they spoke were fruit of bad roots.

The prophet Malachi also said in Ch. 3:13-15, "Your words

have been harsh against Me." Can you imagine saying hard and arrogant things against God? The people were rude and disrespectful against God; they murmured about His provision; they accused Him of not being just and good and they despised His Word, worship and ordinances. In verses 14-15, they stated, "It is useless to serve God. From now on, we'll call the proud blessed and the wicked raised up."

It is not useless to serve God! He gives us great rewards and benefits to His servants. God opposes the proud and He gives grace to the humble. God brings the wicked down, not up. When you become disheartened or start to think this way, be careful about what you say every day and be careful what you say about God.

There was a time in Numbers 20 when Moses disobeyed God. Israel was on the move and they did not have any water. The people began to complain about their lack. Moses prayed, and God told him to gather the elders around a rock and Moses was supposed to *speak to the rock* and God would supply water for His people. Moses was angry at the people and he struck the rock with his rod instead of speaking to it, thereby disobeying God. God told Moses, "Because you did not trust Me to show My holiness in the sight of the Israelites, you will not bring this assembly into the land I have given them." In Deuteronomy 3, Moses desired to see the land and he prayed to God about it but the Lord said, "*Do not speak to Me about this matter again.*" God did not want to hear the negativity from Moses' mouth.

Being around negative people is wearisome. They drag you down with their junk and you don't want to continually hear complaining or whining. Positive speech and expectancy will move you forward, out ahead of the pack. Positive people are always more pleasant to be with because they are encouraging and uplifting.

Meditate in God's Word and Fellowship with Him to Develop Sound Speech

God wants His children to develop a habit of speaking what is right and in line with His Word. Everything that the Lord says comes to pass, so He only speaks that which is right, good and according to His nature and character. He wants us to follow His example of good speech.

The Apostle Paul encouraged his young protégé, Timothy, in the right way to speak saying, "Hold fast the form of **sound words**, which you have heard of me, *in faith and love which is in Christ Jesus.*" By hearing what Paul said, Timothy learned how to speak sound words that resounded with faith and love in Jesus and saw the results of his words. With the help of the Holy Spirit who lives in us, protect the Good News that has been entrusted to you,1 Timothy 1:13-14.

God wants you to establish and maintain a good habit and pattern of sound words. You must decide to speak right your whole life beginning now. The Bible is full of sound words and as you read, meditate and study it, your words will become God's good words and they will please your Heavenly Father. Bible meditation studies the Word of God continually until one can speak it confidently.

Meditation of the mind functions like the digestion of your stomach. With digestion, the food you eat is broken down as you bite, chew, and swallow. It enters the digestive organs and it travels throughout your digestive system. The good benefits of the food are extracted and dispersed through your body and the waste is eliminated.

With meditation, God's Word, your spiritual food, is processed by hearing God's Word with your ears, pondering it over and over with your mind and speaking it several times. God's Word renews your mind which helps you catch God's thoughts and moves into your spirit where it transforms your life. God's Holy Spirit will also help you to change and expand your vocabulary as you meditate on Scripture. Sound words produce a sound life that exceeds limits and crushes barriers.

Meditating on Scripture is also a way to fellowship with Jesus because Jesus is the Word of God. All that Jesus did in His life, on the cross and after He rose from the dead was for us all to have a relationship with God through Jesus. He wants to be involved in your life. Interact with Jesus by talking with Him, sharing with Him and listening to Him. Being in His presence will transform your life.

Remove the Filth from Your Mouth

The words that you use should reflect truth, justice and peace; not lies, injustice or trouble. Systems like a well-water system or a heating system have filters that need to be changed periodically. Filters stop bad things from passing through and improve the quality of the water and air for people to receive the maximum benefit.

Your mouth should also filter out the bad words so good words can pass through.

The filters of your mouth are the contents of your heart and mind. God's Holy Spirit and His Word are components that help monitor your filters and notify you when your filter needs to be replaced.

A good way to remove filth from your mouth is to guard and cleanse your heart from all evil with God's Word and His Holy Spirit. Evil clogs your filter quickly. The prophet Zechariah sums it up this way, "These are the **things you must do**: **Speak truth to one another**; make true and sound decisions within your gates. 17 **Do not plot evil in your hearts** against your neighbor, and do not love perjury, for *I hate all this*" — this is the **LORD's declaration**." Zechariah 8:15-16

Before Jesus, everyone's heart and mind was clogged with junk and our atmospheres were polluted with evil words and deeds. Those who believe in Jesus Christ as Lord, now have truth filters that stop lies and righteous filters that stop evil. Notice the content of the heart and mind are changed because the filth is filtered out.

You must filter out negative, false and hurtful words so that positive, true and helpful words can fill your environment. It says in Ephesians 4:29, "No foul language is to come from your mouth, but only what is good for building up someone in need, so that it gives grace to those who hear." Your mouth filters should prevent you from speaking foul language. Foul language goes against God's standard. You clearly can choose what words you want to use.

Sin corrupts your communication, but God's Word cleanses your communication. Corrupted speech limits you because it is negative, evil and false talk that emphasizes death, darkness, deception and self-indulgence. When you speak like God wants you to speak, obstacles are removed that once held you back. You speak words that are pure, lovely, positive, accurate and truthful. Your words build others up and you go up with them. Only unpolluted and uncorrupted words can change the world which has been corrupted by sin, Ephesians 4:25-32..

4 THE DARK SIDE OF THE TONGUE

Forever Limited and Always Bound. Do not allow your tongue to be used as an instrument of darkness and evil.

There are two powerful forces at work in the tongue, life and death. A dark and evil tongue produces death in whatever it says. A godly and righteous tongue produces life in whatever it says. Proverbs 18:20-21 says, "From the fruit of his mouth a man's stomach is satisfied; he is filled with the product of his lips. **Life and death are in the power of the tongue**, and those who love it will eat its fruit." The New Living Translation translates this verse this way: "The tongue can bring death or life; those who love to talk will reap the consequences."

Speech is the picture of the mind. Your tongue guides your life to a good or bad destination. Words can sway your life in either direction. The tongue is the instrument of either a great deal of good, or of a great deal of evil. Just as there are two sides to a coin there are two sides to your tongue, good and evil or light and darkness. The dark side of the tongue is the negative side of the tongue, which makes God your enemy and causes bad things to happen in your life.

It is the Lord's desire that you keep your tongue from evil and your lips from speaking deceit. He wants you to depart from evil and do good, Psalm 34:11-14. An evil and deceitful tongue is a dark tongue. God is light and there is no darkness in Him and His light can drive out all darkness. Darkness limits and light is unlimited.

A Dark Tongue Can Cause Damage

The dark side of the tongue brings havoc to your life by speaking evil words. It leaves a trail of destruction that can be traced back to the words that were spoken. Following are just a few examples of the destruction caused by a dark tongue.

A dark tongue seeks to devour its victims. It is like a

sharpened razor devising destruction and working treachery. Did you know that you could sin with your mouth? Psalm 59:12-13 reveals that the proud are known by their sinful mouths and prideful words. Proud speech from a proud heart will devour you.

A king in Babylon, Nebuchadnezzar, spoke boastful words about how great *his kingdom* was and how *he built it*. This proud king was cast down and made to eat grass like a cow. That is quite a fall. (Daniel Ch. 4)

A dark tongue seeks to defame you. The wicked, rebellious and evil people sharpen their tongues like swords and bend their bows to shoot their arrows, bitter words at the innocent. It is their intention to drag their name through the mud and destroy their reputation. Satan constantly accuses God's children to get them to quit following God. Don't believe what he says, Revelation 12:10.

A dark tongue causes you to stumble. Evil people encourage themselves in evil plans. They brag about being smarter than anyone else and say that no one can stop them. God will make them stumble over their own tongue, Psalm 64:1-8. Many criminals have said the same thing until they were caught, found guilty and sentenced to prison.

A dark tongue wants you to compromise your belief in God. A wicked and deceitful mouth lie about the righteous. They surround them with hateful words to try to get the righteous to compromise, Psalm 109:1-4.

A dark tongue wants to trap you. Sometimes you can trap yourself with your own words. For some people, it is difficult to say no. The inability to say no can cause friends to regret and resent each other. For example, if you cosign a loan for someone you know or enter into a verbal agreement with a stranger, you could become trapped by your own words. God does not want you trapped so He instructs you to humble yourself quickly, go to the person you entered into that agreement with and try to get released, Proverbs 6:1-5. Being trapped by your words will certainly limit your life.

A Dark Tongue Speaks Dishonest Words. The Lord

considers dishonest words worthless and wicked. Dishonest people go around winking and making gestures to deceive. They distract you with their body language to try to get you to overlook their lies. A dishonest heart is perverse, plots evil and stirs up trouble. They will experience disaster suddenly, Proverbs 6:12-15.

God hates and detests tongues that lie, false witnesses that give false testimony and people who spread strife among brothers. God shares with us things that He hates so we can avoid doing those things. God is truth and He fiercely opposes all forms of lying. God hates the dark side of the tongue.

A Dark Tongue Says Wrong and Negative Things. We live in a dark and negative world. When you focus on negativity it infects your heart and mind and it pours out of your mouth. Remember your heart and mouth are connected. Negative words pollute your life and make you toxic. God opposes negative talk. A dark tongue limits what God can do in your life and restricts you from moving forward in His kingdom. The Bible tells of how people were hindered, hurt and destroyed by the words they spoke.

The good news is, the Lord has equipped you to resist darkness with His light. God's Word is the Light of the world and it can create a new clean heart. A changed heart is the root that produces different fruit. Remember the story of Zechariah? English churchman, Thomas Fuller said, "Learn to hold thy tongue; five words cost Zechariah forty weeks of silence."

A dark tongue uses foolish words. The following are insights from Proverbs 18 about how the dark side of the tongue expresses foolishness.

A dark tongue is antagonistic. In v. 6, a fool's lips lead to strife, and his mouth gets him in trouble. Strife is darkness that invites all wickedness to come in and join it. A dark mouth is a contentious mouth that always wants to argue and fight. Darkness limits and binds you, but light surpasses limits and frees you to move forward.

A dark tongue will ruin you. In v. 7, a dark mouth leads to ruin and his lips are a trap for his life. If you don't change your negative speech into positive speech, it will ruin you. Darkness devastates and confines you. Do you like being or feeling trapped? You can prevent yourself from devastation and being trapped simply by changing the words you use. Different words require a different heart.

God's tongue is light that opposes darkness. God helps you overcome darkness with the light of His Word. God wrote an abundance of good words in the Bible. You can read it and discover what God thinks about any subject or any area of life. It is the supreme book that transforms your speech and sets you free from all traps.

A dark tongue gossips. In v. 8, the Bible describes a dark tongue as a gossiping tongue. A gossiper is a slanderer, whisperer and a talebearer. A gossip passes on stories of others whether true or untrue and likes the attention he gets when people listen. God is against gossip and punishes the one who gossips unless he acknowledges his wrong and asks for forgiveness.

A dark tongue speaks too soon. Finally, v. 13 describes a dark tongue as one that answers before he listens. God calls this foolishness and a disgrace for him. Think of the mistakes that can be made if you do not get all the information you need to make a good decision because you did not listen. A poor listener limits themselves greatly. This is like a person who answers a question on a game show before hearing the full question and completely answers incorrectly. Not listening well can be very costly, Proverbs 18:1-13.

A dark tongue gives an evil report. Our world today is full of negative reporting that is meant to sway opinions in a certain direction, usually against God. The Lord considers a negative report an evil report that is designed to limit, restrict and bind you from possessing what God has given to you. Sin encourages and enhances evil reports which cause people to not look to God nor trust His Word but be bound and lose in life. Evil reports flow out of the dark side of the tongue.

The harmful effects of an evil report are recorded in Numbers Ch. 13-14. God delivered Israel from the bondage of Egypt in a great and powerful way. Some of those who were in Egypt probably doubted whether or not they would break free from the barriers of slavery, but with God they did. God specializes in surpassing limits and carrying out miraculous breakouts.

God always planned for His people to leave Egypt and enter a rich, fertile and large land of their own which He had given them. They were on the verge of this great endeavor. God told Moses to send twelve spies into the land, so they could see with their own eyes that what He had said about the area was true.

Moses obeyed the Lord and sent the spies into this new territory. They spied out the land for forty days and came back to report what they saw. The spies brought back word about the land and fruit that they gathered. In verse 27 they said, "It truly flows with milk and honey and this is its fruit." Their report was good so far, but it was about to go dark.

It is important to see that one sentence was spoken in verse 27 about the good of the land. But in verses 28 and 29 much more was said about the problems they saw in the land. More words were used to describe the potential problems than were used to magnify the goodness of the land. When that happens, you begin to turn to the dark side of the tongue. You can create a problem with your words when no problem exists.

Caleb, a faithful servant of God and one of the twelve spies, tried to quiet the people and silence the dark side of the tongue. He used *words that were from the opposite side of the tongue* and said, "Let us go up at once and take possession, for we are well able to overcome it." God said that Caleb had a different spirit, a positive one.

The other spies who went with Caleb continued to promote the dark side and said, "We are not able to go up against the people, for they are stronger than we." There were tens spies who reverberated a negative report. Now these spies spent forty days searching out the land and nothing happened to them during that time. They entered the land, traveled to different locations and returned to base camp unharmed and free. They did not encounter the strength of the people in the land, they only assumed something to be true that was false. Falsehood and lies influence a dark tongue to limit and bind it. A truthful tongue breaks the chains of lies and makes you free.

The negative report of the ten spies progressed like a blazing fire and infected the whole multitude of people minus a handful of believers who maintained a good report. Their report focused on the size of the fortified cities, the strength of the people, the presence of giants, how the land devours its inhabitants and their own insecurities and inabilities.

Negativity had advanced quickly and deteriorated the faith of many. The people chose to accept the negative and false report of the ten over the positive and true report of the two, Joshua and Caleb. When the people accepted the negative report they cried, complained, spoke against leaders and authority, began to promote death, made themselves victims and desired to get rid of the leaders God had given them. They stated that bondage and slavery were better than freedom and God's will, Numbers 14:1-5. When darkness overtakes a person's mind and mouth it turns into rebellion and incites people to murder, verses 9-10.

God spoke strongly against the dark side of the tongue. He said the people rejected Him, disbelieved Him and denied the signs and wonders He did among them. He intended to destroy them had it not been for Moses' prayer for them. These people despised God, spoke evil words and they did not trust God. When you speak like that over time, refusing to change, it will lead to destruction.

You must know that the devil is behind every deed of darkness, but 1 John 3:8 says "Jesus came to destroy the works of the devil." God, His Word and Spirit are Light and it is the only thing that can overcome darkness. You know that if you turn on a light in a dark room, the darkness flees. Make the darkness in your life flee by turning on God's light and speak His Word.

What we can learn from this true story is that words were used to form two opposing opinions, one positive and one negative. Most of the people chose the dark picture over the positive image. Every person who used their words to complain, lie, speak falsely against leadership and promote death died in the wilderness and did not see the good, rich and fertile land that God promised them.

The dark side of the tongue destroys lives along the way and makes getting to your desired destination much longer, forty days turned into forty years. Negative words produce negative results in your life and positive words produce positive results in your life. Choosing darkness always causes you to be limited and experience loss. God's Word always favors a good report that gives you unlimited breakthroughs.

A Dark Tongue Uses Lies, Flattery, a Double Heart and Pride

People who accept Christ must commit to following Christ their whole life. Jesus described Himself as the Light of the World and if you leave the light of God's kingdom, you will be in darkness. Psalm 12:1-4 describes a time when godly men ceased to be and the faithful disappeared. They **spoke falsehood with one another**, they used **flattering lips** and spoke with a **double or divided heart**. The Lord will eventually cut off all flattering lips and arrogant boasting tongues.

When Paul preached the gospel, he did it as a man approved by God, whom God trusted with His good news. Preaching was a privilege and a responsibility for Paul. When he spoke, his aim was to please God, knowing that God examines the heart. He never preached using flattering words or out of greed. Paul did not seek glory from man, 1 Thessalonians 2:4-7.

The darkness of flattery is it seeks to please men. It uses words that entice people to evil. Through false pretenses, it puffs up the flesh and ego to make them do what it wants. Flattery is very close to manipulation. If you use flattery to get what you want, you are not operating in love and you will fail in the end.

There was a man in the book of Judges named Samson and he had a secret. God had given him super human strength to deliver Israel from the Philistines. The secret of his strength was in his hair which had never been cut. Samson married a woman, Delilah, who was his second wife. She was highly skilled in the destructive art of flattery. His lust for her and her beauty blinded him to what kind of woman she really was.

Delilah was offered a large sum of money by the Philistine

leaders to discover Samson's secret source of strength. She was willing to sell her husband out for money. Flattery was one of the tools that Delilah used to discover Samson's secret. She did not care about Samson's strength, she only wanted to find out his secret to turn him over to his enemies and collect her riches.

In Judges 16:6 Delilah said, "Please tell me, where does your great strength come from? How could someone tie you up and make you helpless?" Notice she compliments his strength and asks how he could be made helpless. She said something nice to do something evil - flattery. Samson toyed with Delilah and lied to her what would render him helpless. Delilah did what Samson said, but it failed because it was not true. That should have been a clue as to how wicked Delilah was, but Samson could not discern her evil intentions. Don't toy with flattery, speak God's Word to it and destroy it.

After making several attempts to sweet-talk Samson, Delilah became more wicked. She questioned his love for her and she nagged him day after day and pleaded with him until she wore him out. Samson eventually told her his secret and she cut his hair when he was asleep in her lap. When he woke up, he didn't even know his strength was gone and he was captured, chained and made blind. Delilah used flattery to destroy Samson. Flattery feeds the flesh, fuels pride and gets you to become self-centered. Flattery flows from the dark side of the tongue. Flattery conquered Samson by stealing his secret.

A Dark Tongue Speaks Deceptive Words

The devil has the darkest tongue of all and uses words to try to deceive people. He is the father of lies and cannot tell the truth if he tried. The devil's main weapon is deception which makes things appear to be different than they really are. A good example of deception is a bomb wrapped in a lovely package. You think the item in the package is good because the package itself looks good. When you open it, you were deceived, because it explodes. Deception is designed to keep you confined and knowing the truth will set you free.

The Bible is the only antidote one can use to stop deception. In Colossians 2:4-8 the Bible warns you not to let anyone deceive you with persuasive words. It's all about the words. You are to guard against deception and you can resist it. Here are some tips to help you avoid being deceived.

- Receive Christ and live in Him for He is truth and light. Deception cannot function in the light.

- Be firmly established and committed to Christ. Put your roots down deep in studying what God said in His Word.

- Remain teachable and be willing to learn about God. Let God's Spirit guide you and be a willing and thankful learner.

- Recognize the enemy's tools of deception of philosophy, empty and meaningless words, traditions of men and principles that are against the Bible.

These tips will help you avoid being deceived.

A Dark Tongue Doubts What God Said is True

Doubt limits but faith breaks barriers. Perhaps you are a person like many that has doubted what God has spoken to you or you have thought that what He said is so incredible that you wondered how it could ever be true for you. A person who doubts believes a negative report more strongly than a positive report. A doubter does not believe that things can change and become better.

Doubt hinders your vision by not letting you see beyond your problem. It causes you to remain focused on your present circumstances and if you doubt long enough, you will lose hope. You can overcome the confinement of doubt by choosing to agree and believe what God's Word says.

The father of our faith, Abraham, went through a brief period when he doubted God. God was patient with him and helped him get past his doubt and into faith. God had promised Abraham that he would be a father of many nations, but for this to happen he needed to have a child. After many years, what God said had not yet come to pass.

In Genesis Ch. 15:1-6, God told Abraham not to be afraid and that He was Abraham's shield and great reward. Abraham responded to God and said, "Lord what can you give me, **seeing I am childless** and the heir of my house is Eliezer, my servant, of Damascus." Did you notice what Abraham was focusing on? He was fixed on his childlessness and not God's promise and that was causing him to doubt God. His eyes were on the wrong thing. Abraham told God that He did not give him an offspring and basically doubted God's promise to him. Other things that God spoke to Abraham came to pass so Abraham knew that God's Word was true. To overcome doubt, you must focus on God's promise more than anything else.

God knew that He could help Abraham overcome his doubt and He worked with him. God assured Abraham that his servant would not be his heir, but one that would come from him and Sarah. Then God showed Abraham the stars and the sand and said that his children would be that numerous. When Abraham saw that picture and heard God's assurance to him, he chose to believe God. His faith caused him to be made righteous.

Abraham's words gave evidence to what consumed him in that moment, his natural circumstances. His focus led him to become frustrated and he struggled with whether or not God's promise was true and for him. With God's patience and encouragement, he cast off the limits that doubt had set up, broke through the barrier that blocked him, and eventually became what God said about him, a father. The words that God spoke to Abraham moved him from unrighteous to righteous and positioned him to exceed any limit.

A Dark Tongue Wavers

One who wavers never exceeds limits or breaks barriers because he can't make a strong decision but wants to hold onto two different opinions at the same time. Indecisiveness breeds instability. A wavering person is like driftwood that is at the mercy of the waves of the sea and the wind and cannot choose which direction to go. He is simply tossed here and there with no direction. The Bible even says that **one who wavers should not**

expect to receive anything from the Lord, James 1:7. A waverer lives within the limits of their indecisive words.

Just as Abraham broke free from his doubt, he also exceeded the limits of wavering. Abraham was tempted to waver between God's promise of being a father of many nations and the childlessness that he and Sarah experienced. If he tried to hold onto God's promise and his childlessness at the same time, that would be wavering. When God gives you His word, you must hold onto that and nothing else. Only when you get a hold of what God said and let go of everything else that may contradict what God said will you exceed limits and break barriers.

Abraham exceeded limits by believing God. The book of Romans 4:13-20 gives us insight about how Abraham did this. Abraham began to say what God said about him. He embraced God's promise by speaking God's Word daily. In verse 20, the Bible says, "**He did not waver** at the promise of God through unbelief but was strengthened in faith, giving glory to God and being fully convinced that what God had promised He was also able to perform."

It is clear how you can surpass obstacles by saying what God said: fully embrace His promises, have strong faith, give glory to God and be fully persuaded in God's ability. Wavering is a dark path that will only restrict you in life. Look to God's Word continually to become fully persuaded that what He said is true and your faith will propel you from impossible to possible.

Another example of the dark side of wavering. Have you ever sincerely asked God to move on your behalf and then circumstances became worse? Be aware in that moment because the enemy of your faith will tempt you to waver to try to get your focus off God, on to your circumstances and get you out of faith.

This very thing happened to a religious leader named Jairus in Mark 5. Jairus heard wonderful reports of the things that Jesus was doing everywhere He went. He heard how people were helped and healed. The testimonies of Jesus were true and Jairus believed God. He was convinced that Jesus could exceed the limits and break the barriers that show up with sickness and disease.

One day, his twelve-year-old daughter became very sick, near death. Jesus happened to be in the town where Jairus lived. Based on what Jairus heard about Jesus, he came to the Lord, worshiped Him and asked Him to come and lay His hands on his daughter so that she will be healed and live, Mark 5:23.

This is an important point: *Jairus used good positive words in making his request*, and *Jesus agreed with him* because He went with Jairus to do what Jairus said. If Jairus' words were dark, doubtful and wavering, Jesus would not have gone with him.

While Jesus, Jairus and a crowd of people were almost at Jairus' house, a servant came out and said, "Your daughter is dead. Why trouble the Teacher any further?" Jesus heard the servant's words. The bad report made Jairus struggle between two opinions. He was tempted to waver from what he originally said to Jesus, about his daughter's healing and his daughter's death. Jairus experienced the full spectrum of the emotions and feelings of that moment. What would he choose to do? Would he accept the limited and bound reality of death or would he remain strong with his original request?

Jesus helped Jairus exceed the limits that were facing him. In verse 36 Jesus responded to the words that the servant spoke and told Jairus, "Do not be afraid, only believe." That is how you break the barrier of doubt and wavering, you resist fear and stick with what you believe about Jesus.

Jesus entered Jairus' home while many were sad, crying and wailing, and **Jesus told everyone that Jairus' daughter is not dead**. The people ridiculed Jesus, so He put them all out of the house.

The Word of God is greater than circumstances, greater than the words of the multitude and greater than death. There is no limit that God's Word cannot go beyond. God's Word changed the atmosphere of Jairus' house. It will do the same for you too.

Jesus put His hands on the young girl, she was healed, and she lived. **When your words agree with God's words, God will**

do what you say.   Do not yield to the temptation to waver. Choose God's side and stay on His side no matter what your circumstances look like and you will reach greater heights and take more ground.

DOUGLAS PYSZKA

5 FLUSH OUT THE NEGATIVITY OF YOUR LIFE

It is important to unclog your life from negativity by flushing it out with something positive like God's Word.

After learning about the dark side of the tongue, you may not want to continue. I assure you, it gets better. To improve the growth of a garden you need to prepare the soil and pull the weeds. The previous chapter did that. Now you are ready to develop further.

Whenever you seem to be stuck in an area of life, you must seek God to help you. If you remain on your own, you will never get free and you will remain bound. It is like someone who is addicted to a substance like a drug or alcohol. Those substances become the rulers of the addict's life. Everything he does is to satisfy those cravings. All the money he gets goes to staying high. He needs help to break free. He undergoes detox to rid his body of those substances. Now he can be renewed.

God frees captives, breaks chains and opens prison doors. Only through His unlimited power can you go past all the limits in this world. God's strength removes all barriers.

It is time to go through a spiritual detox to rid your heart, mind and mouth of the evil of negativity. Controlling your tongue is the key to controlling your body. You must replace evil words with righteous words. To flush out negativity, you must immerse yourself in God's Word through communication with the Lord, study, meditation, confession and action.

To cleanse your heart and mind from the darkness of negativity and evil you need to fill up with something much better. As you fill up with God's Word, all the junk will be washed out. Here are a few practical action steps that will help.

- **Hide God's Word in your heart to prevent sin**, Psalm 119:11. Just as a space suit protects an astronaut from harsh conditions, so God's Word protects you from sin. The Word resists sin.

- **Use your mouth to speak righteous words**. The Bible is full of righteous words, Psalm 71:15. You may want to recall a mother's advice to her children, "If you don't have anything nice to say, don't say anything." Use your mouth to speak good words and don't speak bad words.

- **Proclaim God's conclusions with your mouth**. Meditate and marinate in God's Word. Think about His ways, delight in His statutes and memorize Scriptures, Psalm 119:13-16. Let God's Word flow out of you like water from a fountain.

- **Testify to all the good that God is and has done**, Psalm 119:46. You can use your mouth for good just as it was used for evil. When God does something good, tell others about it and praise Him for it.

- **Abide in the Word of God**. Spend a good amount of time studying it and hearing it, John 15:7. When you change your input you'll change your output.

- **Look for God's Word like someone would search for a treasure**. Celebrate it like you found a gold mine or struck oil in your backyard, Proverbs 4:20-22. The Bible is God's Word, and it is on all forms of media ready for you.

- **Be willing to obey what God said and do it in your life**, Luke 5:5. Obedience to God's Word demonstrates your love for His Word.

- **Trust in God's Word**. God's Word will never change because it is perfect. It is reliable, dependable and trustworthy. He settled it forever in heaven, Psalm 119:89. Nothing else will break down barriers. God never forgets His promises; He sent His Word to you and delivered you from destruction; He revives you with His Word, Psalm 105:8; 107:20; 119:107.

- **Receive God's Word**. Be open to see things from God's perspective. God bountifully supplies those who keep His Word and opens their eyes to see wondrous things, Psalm 119:17-18.

- **Decide to honor, revere and acknowledge God, and He will reward you**, Proverbs 13:13. God honors those who honor Him. God gives great advantages to those who honor Him.

- **Hear God's Word**. Only what God speaks produces faith. Your faith increases in strength by hearing God's Word, Romans 10:17.

- **Renew your mind with God's thoughts**. God's Word is the only thing that can cleanse your heart, soul, mind and conscience, John 17:17.

God has provided a way for you to flush out negativity from your life. He has multiple streams that will cleanse, renew and refresh your entire being. God has good plans for you to bring about the good things He has given to you. When you do things God's way you will reach greater heights and go further than you have ever gone.

6 LIGHT SIDE OF THE TONGUE

You have seen some of the results that come from the dark side of the tongue and have been equipped to flush out negativity. Now you are ready to experience the light side of the tongue which is the positive side.

A light tongue communicates to others. Your tongue is like the pen of a ready writer, Psalm 45:1. Did you know the Bible compares your tongue to a writer's pen? An author's pen is designed to write stories, relay information, record experiences and communicate the author's imagination in order for readers to experience and learn from what the author wrote.

Similarly, your tongue was designed to speak, confess and declare the truth about God into the atmosphere for hearers to discover truth about God. God wants His truth to be proclaimed to every creature, all over the world, so those who hear it can decide to accept it or reject it. Activate your tongue to disperse God's goodness wherever you go.

A light tongue glorifies God. God made your tongue and it is an amazing instrument that really can control your body and direct your life. With it you can glorify Him, promote His kingdom, communicate His love and declare His will.

A light tongue sings to God. Your tongue loves to sing about God's righteousness all day long, Psalm 51:14. The truths about God will excite your tongue more than anything in the world. When you sing about the Lord, joy will resonate with your whole body and God's Spirit will fill you and spill over onto others.

A light tongue's praise is powerful. In Acts 16, there is a story about the power of praise. Paul and Silas were servants of the Lord, preachers, missionaries and apostles. On one of their trips, they encountered a woman who was possessed with a spirit of divination, a fortune teller. Paul cast the evil spirit out of the woman and she was made free. Her owners were not happy because they lost the income they received from her fortune telling. They took Paul and Silas to the magistrates and accused them of troubling their city, Acts 16:20.

The magistrates had Paul and Silas beaten with rods. After they laid many stripes on them, they threw them in prison telling the jailer to keep them secure. The jailer placed them in the dungeon, the worst part of the prison. Paul and Silas were wrongfully accused, hurting in their bodies and in a dark stinky dungeon.

At midnight, Paul and Silas did not complain, murmur or criticize their accusers, but they did something else. **They prayed and sang songs of praise to God**. *They used their tongues to change their situation*. They sang loud enough that the other prisoners heard them. God heard them too.

A great earthquake shook the foundation of the prison and caused all the jail cells to open and every chain to be loosed from every prisoner. Was that a coincidence? No, it was the result of two ministers who sang aloud about God's righteousness. God loved the song so much He tapped His foot and He shook the jail. When you praise God with your tongue barriers are broken, chains are loosed and freedom reigns.

A light tongue learns from God. The light side of the tongue is a tongue that learns, Isaiah 50:4. A great athlete can train his body to do what it needs to do in whatever sport he plays, and you can train your tongue to speak the oracles of God. As your tongue learns, you increase your skill in being able to speak a word in season to the weary and you will see miracles happen.

A light tongue speaks words that reflect God's nature and character. Godly words are a life-giving fountain. Jesus never said anything without substance, power or meaning. His words always gave life, help, deliverance, mercy and freedom to whomever He spoke.

A light tongue prolongs life. How can your tongue prolong life? A tongue that promotes righteousness, holiness, God's goodness and God's purpose of saving the world will extend your life.

Your tongue can control your body to surrender and obey the Lord. Obedience to God prolongs your life. If you keep your tongue from evil you avoid darkness and promote the light. The Promotion of light promotes life and extends your days. If you speak the truth, you speak like God speaks and talking like that prolongs your life. To do what is good, you must have a good heart. God makes your heart good. Producing good fruit prolongs your life, Psalm 34:12-14.

Your tongue is so amazing it can even prolong your life. You may wonder how that works. Nehemiah Adams said, "One of the first things a physician says – Let me see your tongue. A spiritual advisor might often do the same." A short life is a limited life and a long life is a life that has expanded its borders. Your life is prolonged by listening to the Lord and allowing Him to teach you how to honor and revere God. Also, if you delight in life, love a long life and enjoy what is good then **keep your tongue from evil and your lips from deceitful speech**. Stop doing and saying evil things and do what is good. Your tongue influences your life. Do not use your tongue as an instrument of evil or negativity.

Allow the light of God's Word to shine on your tongue and lighten it up. The light side of the tongue is better than the dark side. Speaking positive words is just as easy as speaking negative words, but one produces better results than the other. Which results would you rather have? Tune your tongue to God's frequency, get on the same page as Him and experience His goodness and shatter barriers.

7 VOICE ACTIVATED BARRIER BREAKERS

The words you say and the way in which you praise can turn things to your favor.

The voice of faith. God's Word in you fuels your faith, ignites your praise and changes your life. The only substance in the universe that produces faith is God's Word. Faith comes by hearing and hearing God's Word. Knowing what God's Word says and realizing how good God is, inspires you to proclaim God's praise. You praise Him for choosing you, forgiving you, resurrecting you, calling you, empowering you, leading you and bringing you into His family, 1 Peter 2:9-10.

The voice of praise. A person with strong faith is someone who gives powerful praise to God. Songs, declarations and words of praise are a high form of prayer. Jehoshaphat, a king of Judah, sent out a praise team before his warriors in a battle against three other armies. As they were praising, the three armies that attacked Jehoshaphat turned against themselves and killed each other. Their praise was so powerful it won the battle and they did not even fight. All Jehoshaphat and his army had to do was gather the spoils of victory, 2 Chronicles 20. What do you think will happen in your life if you praised God like that? The next problem you encounter, go around your house praising the Lord proclaiming how good and great He is and watch what happens to your problem.

Discovering the truth that God redeemed you causes great **rejoicing, singing** and **talking** of God's righteousness all day long. If you know God, you cannot remain silent, but you will **speak of** the glory of His kingdom, power, mighty acts and His glorious majesty so others can know it, Psalm 71:23-24; 145:10-12. Praise is exciting, fun and contagious. After announcing what God has done for you, you will begin to shout. The more you praise God, the more you realize how good and awesome He really is.

If you have ever been sad, *down in the dumps* and depressed, God has a cure for you. It is praise. You can remove the spirit of heaviness by putting on a garment of praise, which counteracts the negative effects of depression. Praise lifts you up and brightens your outlook on life, Isaiah 61:3. Even when you do not feel like praising God, you can give Him a sacrifice of praise and tell Him how thankful you are for Who He is and what He has done. Praise shatters barriers.

The reliable voice. Choose to be a voice for God, say what He said, and power will flow out of you. God encourages you to imitate Him, and He enjoys hearing you speak His Word. To be on right side of wisdom and justice is to have God's Word in your heart. How does His law get in your heart? You must study it, receive it and speak it, *then repeat.* The most important ingredient in sound speech is God's Word, Psalm 19:14; 37:30-31.

Be a discreet voice. Discretion protects a person's dignity. A discreet person can bring correction without embarrassing the person being corrected. It can deal with problems without many people knowing what is happening. A person who uses discretion promotes forgiveness and restoration by giving people an opportunity to change. A discreet man speaks righteous words; stands up for what is right; considers wickedness to be an abomination to his lips; and avoids crooked and perverse words, Proverbs 8:6-8.

Be a voice of truth. God favors the person who speaks the truth, God's Word, in love. Truth stands firm but lies are short-lived. There is nothing to cover up when you speak the truth. A liar must continually lie to support the façade that has been falsely established. Lying will eventually wear you down and destroy you, Proverbs 12:17-19.

Use the right voice at the right time. An encouraging, kind and helpful word makes a big difference in alleviating sorrow and depression. A **word spoken in due season** is very good. Pure hearts **speak pleasant words.** **Pleasant words** are like a honeycomb, sweet to the soul and health to the bones. The right word at the right time is like precious gold set in silver, Proverbs 15:23, 26; 16:24.

People who speak God's Word and praise His name are aligned with Almighty God, protected, satisfied and healed. When you confess God's Word and magnify His name you also increase in understanding and knowledge.

God's strength, power and favor show up in the lives of people who speak truth. God opposes people who speak words reflecting the world's attitude and ways. With God, your words are powerful in producing positive results. With the devil, your words are powerful in producing negative results. Decide whose pattern you want to follow. God's pattern produces the best results.

DOUGLAS PYSZKA

8 CONFESSION, PROFESSION AND DECLARATION

A confession that is based on God's Word is a loaded
weapon that destroys limits and demolishes barriers.

When you confess God's Word your release faith to change your circumstance. A confession is a statement that speaks the same thing, speaks the result and agrees with something. Faith speaks what God says, declares the end result and agrees with God's Word. A believer can confess, "I am more than a conqueror in Christ Jesus.", Romans 8:37. This statement shows that he believes what God said. He says the same thing as God the result, not the current outlook. Good confessions that are based on God's Word will manifest God's power.

As we have seen, the Bible has much to say about your mouth, tongue, heart, thoughts and words. By your words you are limited and by your words you exceed all limitations. Words are used in confessions, professions, declarations and statements. These are the vehicles that transport miracles or mistakes. You determine if you are a success or a failure by the words you use every day.

God values faith-filled words and knows that words form images in people's minds. What is pictured in your mind becomes a reality in your life. If you want to change the picture, you must change the words you listen to and the words you speak.

Jesus, Son of God and Son of Man, is the Apostle and High Priest of our confession. A key component that equipped Him for these positions was that He was faithful to God, Hebrews 3:1-2. Jesus was faithful to God in His thoughts, words and actions. Jesus perfectly and fully imitated God, His Father.

In John 5:19-24 Jesus highlighted how He imitated God. Jesus did what He saw His Father do. He always watched His Father and followed His example. Jesus gives life to people just like His Father does. God gave Jesus the authority and ability to judge all matters. Jesus received the same honor that His Father received.

All who hear the words of Jesus and believe in Him have everlasting life. There will be a time when even the dead will hear Jesus' voice and live.

God expects those who believe in Jesus Christ as Savior and Lord to make good confessions, professions, declarations and statements that reflect His nature, character and words. Do not consider confessions you make unimportant. Become disciplined in what you say and how you say it. Right words spoken make the difference between being limited or unlimited.

According to Romans 10:8, God's message is very close to you, in your mouth and in your heart. God's message is a message of faith. Before you make a confession ask yourself, "What does God's Word say?" Get His perspective before you speak. Faith always exceeds limits and goes beyond boundaries taking you into the realm of the miraculous.

God's greatest gift to mankind is salvation and it is received through a **confession with your mouth**. To be saved, you must believe in your heart that God raised Jesus from the dead and confess with your mouth that Jesus is Lord. It is very simple to do. Jesus also added that everyone who calls on the name of the Lord will be saved. Calling is also something your mouth does, Romans 10:8-13.

If the greatest miracle, salvation, comes to you through confession, why wouldn't other things that God promised you, come to you the same way? *Your confession is a key to your manifestation*. Confession is a natural result of believing. A faith confession confounds your enemy. Confessing God's Word counteracts every complaint about a problem and provides you with a divine solution.

Many people believe what God said in the Bible, but they are not confessing what He said. If you really believe it to be true, your mouth will speak it. Abraham had to call himself a father of many nations, which is the meaning of his name, before he became a father. He confessed what God said he was and became the father that God promised he would be. Abraham's confession made the difference in his situation and it will make the difference in your life also. A lack of confession puts constraints on you and keeps you confined. A bold confession is an outward expression of what you really believe and causes your belief to materialize.

Sin is an obstacle that blocks you from God. Trusting in Jesus with your heart and calling on Him with your mouth is the only way to remove that obstacle and break free. Confessing Jesus as Lord invites Him to lead your life. Jesus will not force His way into your heart, you must ask Him to come in. Confessing Jesus as Lord is the only way to escape death, destruction and hell.

How to Enhance Your Effectiveness in Faith Confessions

A faith confession is acknowledging with your mouth the truth of God's Word. Jesus confessed God's Word effectively and we should follow His example. If God's promises are worth believing, they are worth speaking boldly. God gave you His Holy Spirit to lead, guide, direct and bring you into all truth. He is accessible and approachable. As you train yourself in making good confessions, speak God's Word enthusiastically and joyfully because it is a good and powerful message that will propel you beyond all limits and over all obstacles.

Ultimately, the things we receive and have happen in our lives are a direct result of the words we say. If you guard your lips you preserve your life, but speaking rashly ruins you, Proverbs 13:3. If you guard your mouth and tongue, you keep yourself from calamity, Proverbs 21:23.

Just as limits can be exceeded and barriers can be broken, circumstances in life are subject to change. A good positive confession that is based on God's Word is the key to turning circumstances around. God's Word will not change, therefore it has the power to change the changeable.

You do not have to agree with negative circumstances, obstacles or limits in your life. If you do not like scenery in your life, you can change it and form it into something awesome and wonderful with different words. Your words are the stage hands that change the scene behind the curtain. God did it and you can do it too. When God saw darkness as He was about to bring the world into existence, He did not speak of the darkness, but He said, "Let there be light." The setting of the universe was forever changed. What a powerful confession.

Words influence so many things. Here are just a few things that are affected by words.

- Creation – Words brought things into being, established boundaries for water and informed the sun and moon of their purpose.

- Salvation – God's Word is activated when spoken. Confessing Jesus as Lord moves a person from death and darkness to life and light.

- Deliverance – Demons want to possess people and will only leave when told by someone with authority. Jesus, the apostles and other followers all cast out devils with words.

- Commanding an Army – Armies are governed by commands transmitted with words. Armies must follow the chain of command or chaos will result.

- Songs – Songs are words put to music with a certain rhythm and have the power to greatly affect a person's emotions and feelings.

- Marriage – A man and a woman enter holy matrimony by making promises to each other through the words they say. God values vows greatly and rewards those who keep them.

- Public Speaking – Some People have given public speeches full of words and have changed the course of history and we remember their speeches a long time after they were given.

- Swearing in an Official – People who are elected to public offices make oaths, promise to uphold the standards and carry out the duties of the office in which they serve.

From these examples you get the idea of just how important words are, how they affect every area of life and how they are used matters greatly. Every good confession carries much weight and is supported by good character, true, right and just words.

In Acts 4:13, people saw how bold Peter and John were in how they spoke, what they said and the miracle they performed. They knew they were not educated or trained to do miracles like this one, but they acknowledged that they had been with Jesus. Their time with Jesus empowered their confessions and declarations. By God's power, Peter and John spoke with authority, healed a lame man and did not back down when they were pressured to. They blew all their obstacles away.

Miracles Occurred Through Confession

Your confession brings your beliefs into the realm of reality.

One day a leper came to Jesus with a mixed confession, part of it was good, and part of it lacked confidence. The leper said, "If You are willing, You can make me clean." The leper confessed that Jesus had the ability to heal him and cure his disease; but the leper did not know if Jesus was willing to do it for him. Because he was not confident in the Lord's willingness, he did not speak that part with certainty. Jesus responded quickly and said, "I am willing; be made clean." The leper's disease was cured with Jesus' powerful confession of His willingness to do it for the leper, Matthew 8:2. Leprosy limits and Jesus heals.

In Matthew 8:5-13 a soldier came to Jesus on behalf of one of his servants who was paralyzed and dreadfully tormented. Jesus was willing to come to the soldier's house and heal his servant. The soldier confessed that he was not worthy of having Jesus come into his home. He confessed that all Jesus needed to do was to speak a word, and his servant would be healed. The soldier professed an understanding of natural authority and recognized Jesus' ultimate authority. Jesus marveled at this confession and labeled it a great faith confession, one of the greatest confessions He heard in Israel. That's powerful. The soldier's confession produced great results. His confession removed the barrier of sickness and disease from his servant.

There was a woman in Mark 5:25-34 who was extremely limited in her life. For twelve years she suffered with a bleeding problem. She saw many doctors, spent all her money and was no better, but rather grew worse. Not only was she limited, but she was bound too. It did not look like her situation would change.

Then something happened that changed this woman's life forever, she heard about Jesus. Not having the right information will keep you bound and limited. Hearing about Jesus produces faith in your heart. She now had the right information to change her situation, but she had to do something with what she heard.

The next thing she did after hearing was she came to Jesus. She drew close to Him in the crowd, even though it was unlawful for her to be in that crowd with her condition. Faith will overcome obstacles of culture, rules of society and anything else to get to Jesus. This woman had a strong determined faith.

Next, she reached out and touched his clothes. Faith reaches out and gets a hold of Jesus. Making her way through the crowd and reaching out to touch Jesus was probably physically straining because the blood she lost weakened her.

She made a great confession that manifested her miracle. **She said**, "If only I may touch His clothes, I shall be made well," Mark 5:28. She did what she did because she said what she said. *Her words directed her action and activated God's power and she received what she said*.

Her faith confession followed by her confident action changed her circumstance immediately. She felt in her body that she was healed. She made another confession when Jesus asked the crowd who touched Him. Jesus did not know who touched Him but whoever it was received a power transfer. Jesus told the woman, "Daughter, your faith has made you well..." This was no coincidence; **it was confession**. *An ordinary woman made an extraordinary confession and received a supernatural transformation*. She exceeded her limits with a confession of faith and she believed it so strongly, that her confession and actions met together to produce a miracle.

More Miraculous Confessions

- A man named Bartimaeus was blind and cried out to Jesus loudly and confessed he wanted to see, so Jesus restored his sight, Mark 10:46.

- A Gentile woman came to Jesus for her daughter's deliverance. Her daughter was tormented by a devil. She was persistent, unwilling to quit, not easily moved and got her miracle by confessing that dogs get the crumbs, which brought about her daughter's deliverance, Matthew 15:22.

- Jesus asked His disciples who the people said He was. After several answers, Peter, a fisherman, confessed that Jesus is the Christ, the Son of the Living God. God revealed that truth to Peter and Peter spoke it out, Matthew 16:13.

- Ten lepers saw Jesus on the other side of the street and called out to Him for mercy. Jesus told them to go show themselves to the priests. As they were going, one noticed he was cleansed and came and confessed how grateful he was to Jesus. Jesus sent the leper away telling him his faith made him well. He went from just being cleansed to being saved. His confession took him to another level, Luke 17:11-19.

- Your faith confession alienates you from the world. In John 9:22, the religious leaders of the Jews threatened to kick people out of the synagogue for confessing Christ. One day, Jesus healed a blind man as He made mud and put it on the man's eyes. Jesus told him to wash off the mud from his eyes and when did, he returned seeing.

The pharisees interrogated the man with many questions about who healed him and what he thought about the man who healed him. Even his parents were asked to confirm if this man was their son. The parents were reluctant to give a full answer to the leaders for fear of being kicked out of the synagogue. After testifying about Jesus several times, the pharisees threw the man out. The man's faith was so strong that he made a faith confession even though he was alienated by the world. He did not remain silent even when threatened.

Even in Jesus' day there were many pharisees who believed in Him, but they refused to confess Him, John 12:37-43. They refused to confess Him because they loved the praise of men more than the praise of God. These guys limited themselves for a lack of confession.

Your confession is a picture of what you believe, and when you believe God, you will never be ashamed. He backs you up no matter what condition you are in. Confess Jesus is Lord of your condition and He will move to change it according to what you say.

Confession is fruit.

You are like a tree and your mouth is the fruit your tree produces. Good words that come from a good heart and are full of the Word and Spirit of God is good fruit. Good fruit is when we praise God, confess His name, acknowledge Him and thank Him with a joyful and glad voice, Hebrews 13:15; Psalm 113:1-9.

The good fruit of your lips are words that reflect a true partnership with Christ. Would people in the world notice a difference in the way you speak verses the way they speak? If there is no distinguishable difference, check your fruit because it may not be good. Spoiled fruit tastes and smells bad.

What kind of tree are you? Are you an overwhelmed tree, or are you an overcoming tree? Show what you are by your confession. It is by your confession that you are overwhelmed, and it is by your confession that you have overcome.

Holy Spirit's Confession

There are spiritual forces at work in this world that are divided into two groups: good and evil. The Holy Spirit and angels are the good forces that help you to exceed limits and break barriers. The devil and his demons are the evil forces that seek to bind and limit you. We are to test spirits to determine where they are from. The Holy Spirit and the angels are far more superior to the devil and his demons.

A confession determines the difference. The Bible identifies a spirit from God as one who confesses that Jesus Christ has come in the flesh. Every spirit who does not confess Jesus has come in the flesh is not from God. A spirit that denies Jesus is the spirit of antichrist. Notice, it is the confession of the spirit that reveals the spirit's allegiance, 1 John 4:2.

Many people have claimed to have an encounter with some type of a "divine being". If they have no knowledge of how to test which side this so-called being is from, they could be deceived. God told us to test a spirit by what it confesses about Jesus. If the being says anything negative or untrue about Jesus, like He is not God's son, it is a demon promoting a false message. Do not take to heart anything it says. False religions and cults have been formed because a person saw and heard an evil spirit not knowing it was evil. Many people all over the world are trapped in groups like this and they need to be delivered with the good news of Jesus Christ.

The Holy Spirit and Jesus share the same nature, they are both God. Jesus, Who was anointed by the Holy Spirit, also baptizes all His followers with the Holy Ghost and fire. Jesus said, "When the Counselor comes, the One I will send to you from the Father – the Spirit of truth who proceeds from the Father – He will **Testify** about Me." Notice the connection: Father – Holy Ghost – you – Jesus. The Father gets the Counselor to you through Jesus. When the Spirit comes to you, He confesses truth about Jesus.

The word testify is a form of public confession. Strong's Concordance defines it this way – to bear witness, give evidence, and give a good report. The Holy Spirit always gives a good report about Jesus. He will never say anything bad about Jesus.

The Holy Spirit is a personal Mentor, Trainer and Teacher. His job is to bring you into all truth. He doesn't speak on His own, but He speaks what He hears and declares to you what is to come,

John 16:12. He knows your future and He can get you there. If you were to consult a medium, palm reader, or an astrologist, you would be led astray because the spirits behind them are not from God. Evil and false spirits will surely limit you and hinder you. God's Holy Spirit will lead you to greatness.

There are many people who are limited in life because they do not know their purpose or God-given assignment. The spirit of the world is evil and wants to steal from you, kill you and destroy you. If you have accepted Christ as your Savior, you do not have the spirit of the world, but the Spirit that comes from God. Only the Holy Spirit can help you understand what God has freely given to you. God's Holy Spirit will help you understand the Scriptures since He helped write them, 1 Corinthians 2:12-16. You can only discover your purpose and assignment with the help of God's Spirit. Undiscovered purpose produces a limited life. Don't be limited, get the mind of Christ, God's Holy Spirit and go beyond the mark.

The Connection Between Faith and Confession

Confession and faith work together to uproot you from defeat and bring you to victory. The words you confess are the things you really believe. Faith is not silent but speaks with boldness, confidence and certainty. Romans 10:8-13 reveals the connection between believing and confessing. Faith works when the confession of your mouth agrees with the belief in your heart. These two parts work together to manifest your miracle and deliver to you what you desire from God.

You must believe God's Word with your heart. Your heart must embrace, trust and rest on God's Word alone. Do not mix anything else with it or your faith will be polluted and ineffective. When your heart believes, your mouth is ready to speak. It boldly confesses what you believe.

Many people fall short of their miracle because they speak too soon and speak negatively. If you speak when you believe your circumstances more than what God said, your circumstances will either remain the same or grow worse. Remember the woman with the issue of blood in Mark 5? *Her situation changed when she heard and said something different.* She could only change what she said when she changed what she heard and believed. For twelve years she may have believed what the doctors told her, but her condition only worsened. She changed what she heard, believed it, said it, and she was healed.

A strong belief comes from hearing and hearing God's Word and speaking the same thing out of your mouth. Personalize God's Word that you hear by saying things like, "I am victorious. If God is for me, who can be against me..." When your heart and mouth completely agree and say the same thing as God said, power is released, and things change.

When your heart and mouth disagree, that disagreement short circuits the power to change and produces a power outage. It may only take a slight adjustment to get them on the same page and restore power. When your heart and mouth agree, your words are powerful.

For example, if someone is sick, they may hear Isaiah 53:5 which says, "...You are healed by His stripes." They believe that Scripture to be true and agree with it wholeheartedly. Then, they can boldly say, "By His stripes I am healed." Healing is theirs and sickness leaves. Seeing the simplicity of faith and how it works, you know that exceeding limits is easier than you think, and you are right. Your mouth is the master key to change.

The Spirit of Faith

God's Word is like gold, and when you deposit it into your heart, you become rich. Christ-followers have God's treasure in them that the excellence of the power may be of God and not them, 2 Corinthians 4:7-18. The world tries to limit you with lies and pressure; crush you with cares; perplex you with puzzles with missing pieces; persecute you by using people's hands to strike you down. But with the spirit of faith, you overcome all this victoriously and come out from these attacks unscathed.

Have you ever wondered what the spirit of faith is? The spirit of faith unites and harmonizes with the written Word of God. It does two things with Scriptures: it believes them and confesses them as they are written. The spirit of faith knows it will be raised up just as Jesus was raised up. This characteristic of strong believers does not quit and cannot be defeated. The spirit of faith does not lose heart because it is being renewed inwardly day by day. A person with this attitude looks at life and considers it a light affliction, which is only but for a moment; but it knows there is a far more exceeding weight of glory ahead.

Finally, the spirit of faith focuses on the unseen more than the seen. The unseen is eternal, and the seen is temporary. Get a hold of the spirit of faith and let it get a hold of you and watch barriers break before you.

Tips to Make a Good Faith Confession

- Anchor your belief in God. Strong beliefs that rest on a solid foundation make powerful confessions. Only a truth-filled confession based on God's Word can counteract a negative confession. A good confession comes out of a strong belief.

- Believe in your heart. Your confession changes things when you believe what God said in His Word with your heart. Your heart is really your spirit, the real you. Believing with your heart affects your soul, understanding, will, affections and emotions.

- Speak in Jesus' name. There is no greater authority than His name. To use His name, you must believe in Him. Believing in Jesus is acknowledging Him as God's only Son, beholding His glory, fullness, ability and willingness as Savior and Lord to help you.

- Praise keeps your confession strong. Faith in God connects your soul to Christ, the Anointed One, and helps you enter His presence through worship.

- Accept God's qualifications. He qualified and equipped you to make good confessions. Believing God causes you to receive His nature. You are righteous through His righteousness; you are holy through His holiness and you are God's child.

- Know who you are. Your confessions get good results because you realize you are redeemed, chosen, righteous, forgiven and purchased by God. Accepting your position in God gives you a powerful voice.

Confessing Christ

Do not be ashamed of the gospel of Christ for it is the power of God to salvation to all who believe, Romans 1:16.

The best confession you could ever make that leads you to live a life beyond limits and breaking barriers is to confess Jesus Christ as Lord of your life. Acknowledging Jesus as Lord initiates Salvation and a full array of benefits from God. Confessing Christ is an open acknowledgement of **who He is**, He is the Son of God; **what He said**, He speaks the Words of God; and **what He did**, He gave Himself to free you from sin and bring you into His family.

When you confess Christ, you ascribe the whole of your salvation to Him, you give Him the glory of it and you surrender all. Your confession of Christ must be open and in the presence of others. It must be filled with real, heartfelt and sincere words that agree with what you believe in your heart. Philippians 2:11says, "Every tongue should confess that Jesus Christ is Lord, to the glory of the Father."

When you first confess Christ, He comes into your heart and life. You must then hold fast to your confession of faith even if it means suffering a loss of property, liberty or your life. There have been people throughout history who have suffered great persecution for refusing to deny Christ. You must love Christ more than material things or anyone else. When you love Him in such a way, your mind, heart and affection are set on things that are above where Christ sits at the right hand of God and your confession is delivered with conviction and confidence. A life without God limits your potential, is unsatisfying and leads to hell. A life with God takes you to the top.

No one should be ashamed of the name of Jesus. A public confession of Jesus gives you a private audience before His Father, God. A public denial of Jesus denies you access with God, Matthew 10:32-33.

The Bible encourages you to have faith in God, Mark 11:22-24. Jesus is the object of your faith, the source of your faith and the confession of your faith. Jesus is the High Priest of our confession, Hebrews 3:1, and He is the Word made flesh. Faith in God acknowledges God in all your ways and in all you do so He can direct your paths. A faith confession based on God's Word permits God to give you direction.

Faith in God enables you to remove obstacles in your way by speaking to them. God's Word authorizes you and encourages you to speak to mountains which are things that hinder your progress. You can tell them to get out of your way and send them into the sea where they are never seen again.

Faith leaves no room for doubt. If you are going to make a faith confession, you cannot doubt in your heart. You must fully believe that when you make a Bible-based confession, you must believe that when you speak, what you say will be done no matter what.

God's Word Translation says Mark 11:23 this way, "I can guarantee this truth: This is what will be done for someone who doesn't doubt but believes what he says will happen: He can say to this mountain, "Be uprooted and thrown into the sea," and it will be done for him."

If you doubt, you do not believe and if you believe, you do not doubt. Doubters are limited, but believers abound.

Confession Leads to Possession

The life of faith includes a fight. A person who has faith in Jesus Christ will possess a fighting spirit. The fight of faith is a good fight because faith always wins. This spiritual conflict has three parts according to 1 Timothy 6:12; know there is a fight, so get ready; get a hold of eternal life by accepting Jesus as your Lord; confess a good confession before many witnesses, get your mouth moving.

Joshua was a warrior involved in many fights and he dethroned thirty-one kings. God revealed to Joshua an important principle in achieving success in Joshua 1:6-9. God told him to be strong and courageous, observe God's instructions, **speak the law**

continually, meditate in it day and night, and observe it to do it. Joshua learned these principles and implemented them in his life. Speaking God's Word is an important element in winning the spiritual fights you are entangled in.

Live Like Your Confession is True

Your confessions compliment your life and your life backs your confessions. Professing to know God through Jesus Christ must be followed by actively living the way God wants you to live. A profession without corresponding action means nothing. Professing to know God and living in a way that doesn't please Him is abominable, disobedient and disqualifies you from God's promotion, Titus 1:16.

Your confessions and actions must agree and harmonize with each other. Jesus strongly rebuked those who claimed to know Him but lived only to please themselves. If a person's actions always contradict their words, they are unbelievable, unreliable and untrustworthy. When your actions and confessions disagree, you are disqualified for God's work and your life is in disarray.

God honors a good confession. According to 1 John 4:15, when you confess that Jesus is God's Son, God abides in you. God loves to be in an environment where good and sincere confessions are made by people who really mean what they say.

Confession Brings Forgiveness and Cleansing

The Lord knows the frailty of man and He knows that we can miss the mark. Missing the mark limits and restricts our progress. So, God has included in His plan for us the ability to make U-turns in life when we veer off the right path. God's U-turn is called repentance. That means we come to the Lord, confess our sins to Him and He is faithful and just to forgive and cleanse us from all unrighteousness, 1 John 1:9. Our confession corrects our wrong decision and allows us to experience God's love, grace and mercy so we can continue following Him.

God's Confessions Create Good Things

God never asks you to do anything that He has not done. He

abides by His own Word just as He wants us to abide by that same Word. God always makes good confessions that create good things. His confessions are not based on what is seen, but what He desires.

- God looked at the earth that was formless, void and dark, but God confessed, "Let there be light'; and there was light. The Holy Spirit is waiting to bring God's Words that are spoken to pass, Genesis Ch. 1.

- God calls things which do not exist as though they did, Romans 4:17. What He calls into existence begins to exist. God made Abraham a father before he ever had any children, Genesis 12.

- With His confession, God made Gideon, a fearful and small-minded man, a mighty warrior and favored him while he was hiding and threshing wheat, Judges 6:11.

- The Lord called Peter restored before Peter ever denied knowing Him three times. In Luke 22:31-32 Jesus said, "Simon, Simon, look out! Satan has asked to sift you like wheat. 32 But I have prayed for you that your faith may not fail. And you, **when you have turned back**, strengthen your brothers." Jesus confessed he would turn back and He did. Powerful!

- God made Moses into a deliverer while he was a shepherd in the desert, after he fled from Egypt for murder, Exodus Ch. 3.

- Jesus called a storm peaceful and still, and the turmoil stopped, Matthew 8.

- Jesus called a man who was dead for four days to come out of the tomb and the man came out, John 11.

- Jesus called Jairus' daughter not dead but asleep and she was raised up, Mark 5.

- Jesus confessed to a fig tree that no man would eat fruit of it again and it died, shriveling up from the roots, Mark 11.

God makes good confessions that produce good results according to what He says about them. You are created in God's image, enabled to make good confessions, as long as your words and God's words are the same.

Satan is your enemy of faith. He wants to deceive you to keep you out of faith, because he knows you can beat him when you are in faith. Along with deception, another tool that he uses against you is accusation. He is known as the accuser of Christians and the father of lies. When he hurls an accusation against you it is not true. How can you overcome Satan's lies that he hurls at you? You overcome him by the blood of the Lamb and the word of your testimony, Revelation 12:10-12. A testimony is a form of confession. Your confession defeats your enemy and makes you victorious.

God pays attention to the words people speak. Malachi Ch. 3 records that people were complaining against God. They were saying that it is useless to serve God and were calling the proud blessed. All these phrases are very bad confessions. The Lord described these words that were spoken as being harsh against Him. Complainers dishonor God and lie about His nature and character.

On the other hand, in Malachi 3:16, God listened to the conversations of the righteous. He thought so well of them that He recorded them in a book of remembrance. He wanted to preserve the good words that the righteous spoke. When you speak good words about God, His Word and His children, His compassion moves on your behalf and good things are done for you. This clearly shows the difference between a good confession and a bad one.

DOUGLAS PYSZKA

9 DARE TO DECLARE

Those who know God and trust Him are not afraid to open their mouths and declare the righteousness, truth and goodness of the Lord. I dare you to declare!

According to Romans 10:17, faith comes by hearing God's Word and having faith is good, but how do you use the faith that you have? In other words, how do you release faith? How can you exceed limits by using your faith? Having faith is like having a vehicle full of fuel. Simply having a fueled vehicle does not make it go. It needs someone with a key to start it and drive it. The words you speak, the confessions you make and the actions you take drive your faith.

There are two ways to release faith: speaking and acting. **Speak what God said** making it personal and in the present tense – "Jesus, You are God's Son, I receive you as Lord of my life." **Act on what God said** – Jesus told a lame man to pick up his mat and walk. The man acted on what Jesus said and was healed. You must dare to declare what God said boldly and confidently and act your words out. Releasing faith causes you to run past limits and leap over obstacles to get the victory.

As you receive God's Word in your heart, you are depositing His power and treasure in your life. This will help you to overcome any test, challenge or difficulty that arises. When you are pressed by life's circumstances, you can release the power of faith in you by speaking God's Word to avoid being crushed, abandoned or destroyed.

Everything that God does is so good that you want to tell everyone about it. Declare what God has done for you. Begin to extol God with your tongue. If you are serious about overriding the limits in your life then you will make bold declarations about God, Psalm 66:13-16. Bold declarations show that you are not ashamed of knowing God and being associated with Him.

Jesus made very bold declarations. One day, Jewish religious leaders asked Jesus what sign He could show them that would prove He had authority to do all that He did. Jesus declared boldly, "Destroy this temple, and I will raise it again in three days." John 2:18-21. These leaders were thinking about the physical temple they worshiped in, but Jesus was referring to His body which was raised on the third day. He made this awesome declaration before it occurred, then it happened just like He said.

Your mouth is an amazing tool when it is used for God. With your mouth you can speak of God's righteousness, Psalm 71:15; you can declare God's judgments, Psalm 119:13; and you testify about God before kings without shame, Psalm 119:45.

Moses dared to declare God's Word before kings. Moses appeared before Pharaoh in Egypt many times to declare to him, "Let my people go." Pharaoh could not stop him, deter him or even arrest him. God gave Moses power, authority and ability to declare before a king. God favors those who dare to declare truth to others. Moses' declaration brought freedom to God's people and caused them to smash the slave barrier.

People in the world need to hear God's story, His good news. You know the world can use all the good news it can get to counteract all the negative news it gets. Believers in Christ are to declare God's glory among the nations and His wonders among the people, 1 Chronicles 16:23-24. Every declaration you make about God, His nature, character and His Word will take you past all limits and over all barriers.

Godly declarations can be separated into three levels. On level one, you declare God's glory, His message and the wonders that He does. You point people to the Lord. On level two, your declaration advances to singing, praising and rejoicing. You express excitement for what God has done for you. On level three, your declaration emphasizes God's nature, character and His Word. You recognize God more clearly and you look, act and sound like Him more.

Level one - Declare what God has done among the people. Recount what the Lord has done to the next generation and declare His righteousness to them who will be born. All people who learned about God at an early age should proclaim God's wondrous works their whole life. Every generation should declare God's story to the next generation because every generation needs to hear about God. The purpose of declaring God's works is so that men will honor and reverence God and consider wisely what they do.

A sick person should declare, "I shall not die, but live and declare the works of the Lord. If God has done something for your soul, declare it! Speak God's good news of salvation publicly every day and declare His glory to the nations. When you face trouble, declare that God delivers you from all trouble.

Level two - While one generation praises God for His works, another generation declares His mighty acts. When you declare what God has done, mention that His name is above every other name. No one else has done or will do what God does. He alone is worthy of our praise. All that God does is exciting, and it needs to be proclaimed world-wide.

Level three - Declare the Lord's name to believers. His name is above any other name. No other name can save you from hell. He goes by many names, but Jesus represents all His names. The older believers should declare God's strength and power to the next generation. Affirm God's lovingkindness in the morning and His faithfulness at night. Declare the Lord is upright and speak of His greatness and goodness. People need to know that God has so many good qualities to help them in every area of life.

There is a way to exceed the limits that restrict you in life. The enemy cannot confine you, the world can't stop you and all your insecurities won't hinder you. They will be shattered because you dare to declare good things about God, His Son, His Spirit and His Word.

Personal Declarations

These are just a few suggestions and the tip of the iceberg of what you can declare.

- I am a child of God. John 1:12 - You become a child of God by receiving Him and believing in Him.

- I am more than a conqueror. Romans 8:37 - We are more than conquerors through Him that loved us.

- I am accepted in the Beloved. Ephesians 1:6 - He made us accepted in the Beloved.

- I know what God's will is for me. Colossians 1:9 - Pray that you may filled with the knowledge of His will…

- I have a divine inheritance. Ephesians 1:11 - In Him also we have obtained an inheritance…

- I am forgiven. Ephesians 1:7 - In Him, we have redemption through His blood, the forgiveness of sins, according to the riches of His grace.

- I am loved by God. Ephesians 2:4 - God is rich in mercy, because of His great love with which He loved us.

- I am always victorious. 2 Corinthians 2:14 - God always leads us in triumph in Christ…

- I overcome the accusations of the devil. Revelation 12:10 - They overcame Him by the blood of the Lamb and the word of their testimony.

- I can do all things through Christ who strengthens me. Philippians 4:13.

10 WINNING WITH WORDS

If you want to win in life, you need to speak winning words and act like a winner.

The difference between your defeat and your victory is the words you speak. No one becomes undefeated by being silent. Everyone who believes in God must be prepared to fight. You do not fight spiritual battles with natural weapons, punches or kicks, but you do fight with your words. The way to win the fight of faith is to make good confessions, professions and declarations before witnesses. Train yourself in the Word of God and become a skillful speaker of Scripture.

The simple confession that Jesus is Lord mixed with faith in your heart that He is God's Son, puts you on the winning side of life. God responds to your invitation and He dwells in you. Confessing Jesus as your Lord, and believing it wholeheartedly, changes your course from hell to heaven.

A great example of winning with words is from the story of David and Goliath found in 1 Samuel 17.

The story gives the account of two armies, Philistines vs. Israel, arrayed in battle formation ready to fight each other. Each army was on an opposing mountain looking down onto a valley where the warriors would engage in battle.

Goliath, a champion from the Philistine army, came out onto the battlefield. He stood over nine feet tall and was covered in heavy armor from his head to his feet. He spoke proud, arrogant and provoking words to Israel which were meant to intimidate, confuse and instill fear in Israel's army. His stature and perhaps his reputation added validity to his words.

There was evidence that Goliath's words were working, because when king Saul and all Israel heard Goliath's words, they were dismayed and greatly afraid. They looked at Goliath's size and armor, heard what he said, and they were too afraid to engage him in battle. Goliath's words paralyzed an army because the army had no faith. Goliath intimidated Israel with negative, abusive and mocking words for forty days.

One day of listening to the enemy's nonsense is too long! Shut your enemy up with God's Word quickly. If you heed your enemy, you will be forever limited and restricted by any barrier he builds. You do not have to listen to your enemy no matter their size or what they claim to be able to do. You can beat him with God's words every time. What was Israel going to do? How would they overcome this opponent?

Someone on Israel's side needed to *speak something positive, truthful and in agreement with God's Word* to counteract the enemy's evil words. There was not one trained soldier in Israel who was willing to speak against Goliath. Then God sent them a shepherd who was full of the Word of the Lord.

God sent a shepherd named David to the battlefield to turn the tide of the battle. David was the youngest son of Jesse, who had seven other sons. David's three oldest brothers were soldiers in the Israeli army. David occasionally went back and forth to help Saul and to take care of his father's sheep, 1 Samuel 17:15.

David was there to deliver supplies to his three brothers, their captain, and to find out how his brothers were doing. The two armies were now facing each other. Then, David left his supplies with the supply keeper and greeted his brothers.

While David greeted his brothers, Goliath again spoke his proud, arrogant and provoking words. David heard what the giant said. All the soldiers fled when they saw Goliath because they were dreadfully afraid. Some of them said, "Have you seen this man who has come up? Surely, he has come to defy Israel; and it shall be that the man who kills him the king will make very rich, give him his daughter in marriage and his household will be tax exempt in Israel.", 1 Samuel 17:25.

David spoke to the men near him and inquired about the reward that was promised for killing the Philistine champion. The reward caught David's attention and formed a good picture in his mind of being married to the king's daughter, rich and exempt from taxes. He could see himself possessing those things. He strengthened his belief in receiving the reward by hearing it more than once. *Faith comes by hearing and hearing….*

David immediately identified Goliath as an uncircumcised man, one who defied God and placed him on the losing side. Goliath was not connected to God, did not know God and had no promise from God. David knew that God was for him, and not for Goliath, so David was convinced at that moment that he could defeat Goliath because God was on his side. **David knew this was a spiritual battle and one he could win by faith.**

David's oldest brother Eliab was jealous of David because of how David spoke about the situation. David demonstrated greater faith than his older brother. Eliab was too fearful to speak or take any action against Goliath. On the other hand, David spoke against Goliath and knew that he could be defeated and was willing to back up his words with action. Eliab tried to make David seem small and insignificant to make himself feel better. David paid no attention to Eliab. Don't let fearful people infect you with their fear and cause you to lose your focus on God's assignment for you.

Whenever you face opposition, and we all do, you must speak words that promote victory. Declare yourself to be on God's side by exalting Him and His cause. Boldly proclaim what God can do. David heard what the reward was several times and he had faith to receive it. *David's words brought him before the king.*

1 Samuel 17:31 says, **"David's words were heard** and reported to Saul, and he sent for David." How does a shepherd gain access to the king? David, the shepherd, was summoned by the king because *the shepherd spoke like a warrior*! The king of Israel was attracted and impressed by David's words. **No one else spoke like David**. When David came before the king, he spoke positive, confident and victory-oriented words saying, "Let no man's heart fail because of him, Goliath; you servant will go and fight with this Philistine.", 1 Samuel 17:32. Where do your words send you? What doors do your words open for you? You can change your destination by changing your words.

Those in the world do not understand *faith talk*. Saul doubted David's ability because of his age. David responded and told Saul how he went after, struck and killed a lion and a bear. David spoke as if Goliath was already defeated by equating him with animals that he killed. David declared that the Lord who delivered him from the predators would deliver him from the Philistine also.

If you desire to defeat an enemy, you must *speak against him before you kill him*. The Philistine cursed David to his gods and hurled insults at him saying how he will defeat David. But David stood his ground and spoke back to the giant. He told the giant his secret weapon, the name of the Lord of Hosts, the God of Armies, who Goliath spoke against. David testified how everyone would know it is the Lord who saves with His own weapons and not man's.

Once David won the war of words, he loaded his sling with a rock, swung it and it hit Goliath between the eyes knocking him down. David had no sword of his own, so he took Goliath's sword, cut off his head and made sure the giant was completely defeated. No weapon formed against David prospered. If your enemy aims a weapon at you, it might be used to destroy him.

Here is the important thing to know: **It was the words David spoke that brought this victory to pass**. Everything David said is what he did and what happened. The confessions, declarations and statements that came out of David's mouth broke the barrier that paralyzed an army for forty days and gave Israel an ultimate victory. David won with words first, then he succeeded with the sling and sword. Decide today that you are going to win with words in your own life against the enemies you face.

Imitate God's Speech

Only by God's grace and power can you win in life, but you must develop a new "way to say". You can say things in a better way, using different words that God would approve of. God has won, He wins every day and He will always win because **He wins with His Words**. If you have read the gospels, you can see that Jesus demonstrated this because everything He said came to pass. He predicted His resurrection accurately. He declared how His followers would be treated by those in authority. He never lied to His disciples about anything. You can follow His example of good sound speech. If He won with words, we can follow His example and win too.

You will lose and not win with sin. Many people think that there are levels of sins, some being worse than others. God looks at all sin and considers it all to be bad. In God's eyes, sin is sin. God listed some things that He wouldn't approve of in Ephesians 5:1-5. You may be surprised to know that along with sexual immorality, impurity and greed, God adds coarse, foolish talking and crude joking as unacceptable behavior. Be sure to imitate God when you speak. A filthy mouth is just as much sin as committing murder.

When Christ comes into a person's heart, a new speech pattern develops. You become a new creature in Christ, with a new mouth and you begin to use words that are gracious, preserving and positive. You avoid criticizing others, judging or speaking harshly with the intent to offend. You begin to speak truth in love. With your mouth you limit yourself or with your mouth you shatter records.

Speak What is Right to Honor God

It is right to speak God's Word. People who do God's will and obey Him are successful. Part of their success involves speaking God's Word constantly and consistently. It becomes a good habit when God's Words flow out like a river from their mouths. God's heart rejoices and celebrates when we speak what is right.

It is right to speak life. A godly man's mouth is a life-giving fountain. Life flows to whatever he speaks to. He speaks wise words that are more valuable than gold or precious gems. Your tongue is like a faucet with hot and cold water, so choose which side of your tongue you turn on to determine what flows out of it, the death side or the life side.

It is right to speak faith-filled words, it pleases God. If you want to please God, then live by faith. A person who lives by faith, speaks what is right and makes God's heart rejoice. God applauses a person that has a right heart and speaks right words. Being on God's side eclipses limits and removes blockades in your life, Proverbs 23:15-16.

God favors the righteous and their wise words. One thing that will certainly give you the winning edge is God's favor. God's favor moved Joseph from being a prisoner to the prime minister in Egypt; it helped Esther gain access to her king and save her people; and it caused Daniel to be loosed from lions' mouths and experience great promotion and success. Who does God favor? He favors the **words of a wise man**. Speak wise words and win God's favor, Ecclesiastes 10:12.

Don't let your anger control you. Many people in the world today are overtaken by anger and speak angry words. If anger controls your speech, it will destroy you. The Bible wants you to learn a new language and get rid of all evil behavior - inappropriate actions and responses; all deceit, that uses misleading words; hypocrisy, where words and actions do not agree; jealousy, where you do not trust anyone, but speak suspiciously of everyone. Finally, **stop speaking evil of any kind, don't say cruel things about others or use insulting language**, 1 Peter 2:1.

If you can keep your mouth right, you will keep your life right. Let the words you use in every day conversations reflect the gospel of Jesus Christ. Clearly, there are words that are acceptable to God and there are words that God rejects. The best way to assure that God accepts your words is to learn His Word, Philippians 1:27; Psalm 19:14.

You may not buy into the truth that your words are so powerful and influential, but they are. There was a great king of Babylon in history, named Nebuchadnezzar. He had a very great and vast kingdom, but he was very proud and spoke prideful words. This king was warned by one of his advisors, Daniel, to separate himself from his sins and do what was right. Nebuchadnezzar was given an opportunity to repent and change his heart and words, but he chose not to, Daniel 4.

As the king was walking out on the roof of his palace he said, "Is this not Babylon the great city that *I have built by my vast power* to be a royal residence and to display *my majestic glory*?" The king continued to speak prideful words and magnify himself.

The Bible says, "While the **words were still in the king's mouth**, a voice from heaven said, "King Nebuchadnezzar, the kingdom has departed from you. You will be driven away from people to live with wild animals, and you will feed on grass like cattle for seven years until you acknowledge that the Most High God is ruler over the kingdom of men." Pride-filled words will limit you until you speak humble words.

The king of Babylon spoke words which affected his life in a negative way. God heard what this king said, and judged Nebuchadnezzar's words with His righteous and Holy Word. What God spoke to this heathen king happened exactly as it was told to him. It is even recorded in history that Nebuchadnezzar survived a seven-year bout with insanity. (Ancient History Encyclopedia Joshua J. Mark published on 20 July 2010)

When the seven years were finished and the king's sanity returned to him, he came in from the field looking normal and he also changed his words. He exalted the Lord's kingdom, acknowledged God's power and praised His name and nature. **Different words brought a different outcome**. This king changed from praising himself to praising God. He declared that God's works are true, and His ways are just and those full of pride can be humbled. King Nebuchadnezzar overcame a great loss and turned it into a great victory by saying different words than what he had said before, Daniel 4:24-37.

11 THE IMPACT OF THE WORD OF GOD

"Words must be weighed not counted." Author unknown

The greatest example for us to follow in speaking correctly and saying powerful words is Jesus. His words are forever settled in heaven. Jesus is God's Word in the flesh and He spoke true words, life-giving words, loving words, positive words, corrective words and faith-filled words. Jesus spoke in the Old Testament as well as the New Testament because His words are eternal.

No words ever had nor will have such a lasting impact on the world like the words that Jesus spoke. The good news is that Jesus has authorized and encouraged all who believe in Him to speak like Him. He commissioned us to converse like Him. We can say His words in His name and the same power that operated for Him will operate for us.

The impact of Jesus' words is eternal. Mark 13:31 tells us, "Heaven and earth will pass away but **the Lord's words will never pass away**." Even while Jesus walked the earth, many who heard Jesus speak marveled at the gracious words that proceeded out of His mouth. His teaching astonished people because it was true and powerful. When He spoke, people acknowledged His divine authority. Military officers also recognized how powerful Jesus' words were, John 7:46.

Jesus needed to set things right and repair what man broke when he sinned. God made Him judge over all things. Jesus was and always will be the greatest speaker ever. His words positively impacted people, both individuals and groups, generations, nations and the world.

The Bible uses natural things to communicate to us God's Word is powerful. His Word is like a fire. A fire is powerful. It can remove waste, purify, heat an area, light a path, cook food and protect. God's fire is a holy fire. It cleansed the filthiness of Isaiah's lips, Isaiah 6. It removes the waste of the works of the flesh of man, that are done apart from God. It was a force in

Jeremiah's bones that compelled him to preach, Jeremiah 20:9. A fire led and protected the Israelites as they moved through the wilderness in Exodus. Finally, when God poured out His Spirit on His church He used the symbol of fire as a sign to them. As they were touched with the fire they supernaturally spoke in other languages, Acts 2.

The Bible also describes the word of the Lord as a hammer, Jeremiah 23:29, that pulverizes rock. A hammer is a powerful tool that breaks up hard ground, drives in nails and separates things that no longer need to be together. God's Word breaks up the hardness of a prideful heart and humbles the stiff-necked. Like a hammer driving in a nail, the Lord drives home what He said to increase our understanding. As the claw of a hammer removes a rusty nail, the holy Word of God separates us from things that are no longer good for us or unnecessary for His plan to work.

The word of the Lord is a multipurpose tool that is useful in different environments and can be used in special ways to accomplish what God desires. It works anywhere and in any place.

God's Spoken Word Brought Bones to Life

In Ezekiel 37, The prophet Ezekiel had a vision of a valley full of dry bones. The bones were many, scattered on the ground, unconnected, lifeless and they were dry, perhaps being there for a long time.

The Lord asked Ezekiel if these bones could live. Could the bones become people again? Ezekiel did not know the answer, but he acknowledged that the Lord knew. What would make the dry, scattered bones live? **Simple, speak to them**. The Lord said, "Prophesy to these bones, and *say to them*, "*O dry bones, hear the word of the Lord!*" Prophesy to bones? Yes. To prophesy is simply to **speak what God says**. It is *inspired utterance*. The Lord instructed Ezekiel to speak to the bones and say, "Dry bones, hear the word of the Lord!"

The condition of the bones may reflect some things in your life. You may have many things in your life like dreams, desires and goals that have died, been separated from you and scattered out of your reach for a long time. It is time to speak to those things, resurrect them and reignite them with expectation. The Lord will help you by telling you what to say to them.

Ezekiel then spoke God's Word to the bones and barriers were removed. As he spoke the prophetic message, he heard a noise - (*clack, clack, clack*) and suddenly a rattling; and the bones responded to the word of the Lord that Ezekiel said. The bones started to move into place, each one finding and connecting with its original skeleton. Then, tendons appeared, flesh grew, and skin covered them. Wow, what an impact the Word of the Lord had when Ezekiel spoke it!

There was one more thing that Ezekiel had to do. Standing before him were lifeless people. How could life come into these shells? The Lord commanded Ezekiel to prophesy again to the breath. The Lord told Ezekiel exactly what to say. Ezekiel spoke God's words and commanded the breath to enter them and the lifeless human shells came to life and were a vast army.

When Ezekiel spoke the word of the Lord, the impact was incredible. The situation he saw before his eyes was completely transformed. When you speak God's Word to your dreams, desires and goals, they can become vibrant and full of life once again. Know that God has a word for whatever situation you face too.

He will lead you to speak to it, declare His Word over it and confess a good confession about it. You must open your mouth and God will fill it with the right thing to say. Speaking God's words will dramatically change the atmosphere and environment of your life and cause **you to exceed limits and break barriers**.

God's Plan of Salvation

The best way to exceed limits and break barriers is to make Jesus Christ your Lord and Savior if you haven't already. To become a child of God you must put your faith in Jesus Christ, believe that He is God's Son and ask Him to be Lord of your life. You must surrender your whole self to Him and He will graciously lead you on the right path. He will be with you and dwell in you. He loves you. This is the only way to be certain you will bypass hell and spend eternity in heaven.

12 A SUMMARY OF THE POWER OF WORDS

After reading this book, you may pay closer attention to the words you use every day. Understanding the power of words is very important in breaking free from boundaries and limitations that you encounter in life. You must be committed to changing your words, so you can change the negative circumstances that are facing you. The following are a few highlights of the power of words.

1. Words can poison or destroy. Persuasive words can seduce you and lead you astray, Proverbs 7:21.

2. Good advice leads to safety. There is safety in the multitude of counselors. Some of God's counselors are His Holy Spirit and the writers of the Bible.

3. If you can control your mouth you can protect your life. When you guard your mouth, you shield your life. Wholesome words give life. Talking too much can ruin you, Proverbs 13:3; 15:4.

4. Right words can turn an angry man into a friend and wrong words can turn a friend into an enemy. A soft answer turns away wrath; grievous words stir up anger, Proverbs 15:11.

5. Your words reveal if you are wise or a fool. Wise people speak words of wisdom, but fools speak foolishness. The words you listen to and look at are the words you speak, and they will come to pass in your life. Get advice and instruction from God and you will be wise, Proverbs 15:2; 19:20.

6. Your words can influence your personal happiness. Positive, upbeat and good words can bring joy to you. It is amazing how helpful a word spoken in due season makes you feel good and encouraged, Proverbs 15:23.

7. Foolish words can cause you to fail. The mouth of a fool is his destruction and snare to his soul. Foolish words will come around to bite you. Wrong words can wound others and the lips of a fool lead to strife. Strife brings every other evil with it. Wrong words can wound others. The lips of a fool lead to

strife, Proverbs 18:6-8.

8. Words determines what lives or dies. The mouth is such a powerful instrument that life and death are in the power of the tongue and those who love it will eat its fruit, Proverbs 18:21.

9. Words determine the course of life. If you listen and respond positively to correction you will be on the right course. If you stop listening to correction and resist it, you will get off course, Proverbs 19:27.

10. If you do not control your tongue, it will get you in trouble. A way to avoid trouble is to guard your tongue. Guard your tongue by meditating and studying the Bible and think before you speak, Proverbs 21:23.

11. Your success or failure in life is determined by the timing of your words. Stupid people express their anger openly. They open the spicket full and their anger gushes out too quickly. Sensible people are patient and get all the information necessary before they express their acceptance or opposition to a proposition, Proverbs 29:11.

12. Your words can help the poor and needy. The poor have no voice and need others to speak up for them. Speak up, judge righteously and defend the cause of the oppressed and needy, Proverbs 31:8-9.

13. Your words can trap you. If you agree to do something that you know that you shouldn't do or for a person you shouldn't do it for, your agreement will trap you. Don't agree to cosign a loan for a shady person. The only way to get out of that trap is to go to the person and humble yourself and beg to be released from your obligation, Proverbs 6:1-5

14. Right words can save you. Wicked words are like a surprise attack on the innocent to murder them. The words of the godly save lives and deliver from evil, Proverbs 12:6.

15. Right words and wise words can bring healing. Reckless words pierce a soul like a sword. Jesus is our wisdom and brought healing through the words He spoke everywhere He went, Proverbs 12:18.

16. Right words give you access to powerful and important people. Good rulers detest wicked behavior. Good rulers delight in righteous lips and one who speaks honestly, Proverbs 16:12-1

17. The quality of your words reveals the quality of your heart. Good words come from a good heart. Evil words come from an evil heart. An ungodly man digs up evil and his lips are a burning fire. A troublemaker promotes strife and gossips to divide. Violent people mislead their friends and lead them down a harmful path, Proverbs 16:27-29.

18. Right words will energize and motivate you. Wise words bring you many benefits. God will reward those who speak good things. God is good and when you speak like Him you shall be rewarded, Proverbs 12:14; 14:14.

.

BIBLIOGRAPHY

Dare to Declare Scriptures

(Psalm 9:11; Psalm 22:30-31; Psalm 71:17; Psalm 78:5-8; Psalm 73:28; Psalm 118:17; Psalm 665:16-17; Psalm 96:1-3; Psalm 142:1-2; Isaiah 12:4; Psalm 145:4; Psalm 22:22; Psalm 71:18; Psalm 92:1-2; Psalm 92:15; Psalm 145:6-7).

Antony Farindon - Dictionary of National Biography, 1885-1900, Volume 18

Farindon, Anthony by Alexander Gordon

Maltbie Davenport Babcock - "Thoughts for Everyday Living (1901)" Published December 1st 2008 by Kessinger Publishing

THAYER'S GREEK LEXICON, Electronic Database. Copyright © 2002, 2003, 2006, 2011 by Biblesoft, Inc. All rights reserved. Used by permission. BibleSoft.com

ABOUT THE AUTHOR

Doug Pyszka has a passion to help people know what God has given them in His word. It is their desire to help people discover their treasure and inheritance in God's word and to encourage people to know how anyone can enjoy and experience God's promises in their life.

Doug currently serves as Sr. pastor of Victory Christian Fellowship in Palmyra Pennsylvania. He and his wife, Fiona, have ministered there for sixteen years. Doug has a strong and anointed teaching gift where God brings the gospel to life.

Doug is a 92 graduate of Rhema Bible Training Center in Tulsa, Oklahoma and a graduate of Lee University in Cleveland, Tennessee. You may check out their website at www.vcfpa.org and listen to one of their messages for free.

www.ingramcontent.com/pod-product-compliance
Lightning Source LLC
Chambersburg PA
CBHW060131050426
42448CB00010B/2076